D0901310

Letting Go
With
All
Your
Might

Kim Wolinski, MSW

ReDecisions Institute ™

LETTING GO WITH ALL YOUR MIGHT
A Guide to Life Transitions, Change, Choices & Effective ReDecisions
by Kim Wolinski, MSW

Copyright ©1995, ©2002 2ⁿᵈ Edition Workbook by Kim Wolinski, MSW
ReDecisions Institute

ReDecisions for Life ™, The ReDecisions Model™ and The ReDecisions 11-Stage
Model™ are registered trademarks of ReDecisions Institute.

The publisher offers discounts on this book when ordered in quantity for special
sales. For more information, please contact:
  ReDecisions Institute
  PO Box 6149
  Longmont, Colorado 80501
  www.ReDecisionsInstitute.com

Library of Congress Catalog Card Number: 94-68760
Library of Congress Cataloging-in-Publication Data

Wolinski, Kim, 1956-
  Letting Go With All Your Might: a guide to life transitions, change, choices
  & effective redecisions / Kim Wolinski.
      p. cm.
  Includes bibliographical references.
  1. Change/Psychology 2.Transitions 3. Self-Development 4. Self-
  Management 5. Paradigms
  I. Title. II. Title: a guide to life transitions, change, choices & effective
  redecisions

            3 5 7 9 10 8 6 4 2

All rights reserved. No part of this publication may be reproduced, stored in a
retrieval system, or transmitted, in any form, or by any means, electronic,
mechanical, photocopying, recording, or otherwise, without the prior written
consent of the publisher. Printed in the United States of America.

Permission granted to reprint this excerpt:
From *There's a Hole in My Sidewalk* ©1992 Portia Nelson,
Beyond Words Publishing, Inc., Hillsboro, Oregon

Permission granted to reprint lyrics:
"Kickin' and Screamin'", written by Tony Arata, sung by Garth Brooks, *In Pieces*
album ©1993 by MorganActive Songs, Inc./Pookie Bear Music (ASCAP)

Cover Design by Orbit Design
Illustrations by Art Only (Katherine Townsend) Scanned for 2nd Edition
Text design by MarketAbility, Inc. (Kim Dushinski)
Printed by LightningSource.com
Set in 11 point Clearface by KeyFontsPro
Quick Type Condensed

ISBN 1 885968 07 8

Dedicated to . . .

Mary Adams, my graduate work advisor,
and
Hobe Burch, my Special Studies professor,
who 10 years ago believed in me and my vision.

And, to each of you willing to go into the dark places —through the
dark night — many times over, in order to come back to yourself
more fully and more clearly than ever before. To those who are
willing to live life fully, consciously and deliberately more often
than not.

Acknowledgments

I'm glad that one of my ReDecisions has been to let go of thinking I have to do things all by myself. Many thanks to the following friends and family, colleagues, mentors, teachers and students for their invaluable assistance to materialize one more of my visions.

- To my "right hand," Kim Dushinski, for formatting and helping to create this book and without whom I couldn't do half of what I do.

- To Jane Stumm Cuva, for early editing and who knew me "way back when," when I first said, "I can do this speaking thing!"

- To my brother, Dave, whose observations have made me rethink the use of the apostrophe.

- To Lory Floyd for final copyediting support.

- To Katherine Townsend for her always flexible, brilliant and beautiful creative vision and artful work on this book's cover and illustrations.

- To Gordon Burgett for many hours of expert guidance (and bad jokes) on book writing and publishing.

- To Dan Poynter for guidance through his book, *The Self-Publishing Manual.*

- To Lisa Obroslinski for inviting me to let go of the first title to this book that kept it from being finished.

- To Wes "Scoop" Nisker, another small town Nebraska kid, and his delightful book *Crazy Wisdom*, for inspiring the title of this book.

- To all of the students, workshop participants and clients who over the years have shared with me their life stories, questions and answers.

- To my parents, Don and Marlene, for their love and support and for "breathing through" my *many* life/work ReDecisions.

- To Nanci Griffith and Garth Brooks for singing me through another project.

- To Thomas Moore for writing *Care of the Soul*, one of the major catalysts, in my creating this book.

🙵 To Doug Benson for leaving his porch light on.

🙵 To Ruth McGuire Tuck, Rita Smith, Annette and Kenny Lemon, Jennifer Gore, Jan Hixon, Leav Bolender, Cathy Bassos, Michael Treadwell, Kathy Canclini, Sidney Morris, Marlene Gakle, Dean Kunc, Fritz McCord, Ginny Wilcox, Suzi Bartels, Paula Kucera, Bruce Inness, Natalie and Jeff Feit, Stan Olsen, Sherry Zimmerman, Carol Frederick, Joseph Campbell, Angela Lansbury, Katharine Hepburn, Oprah Winfrey, Gilda Radner, Merle Shain, Richard Bach and many others, much heart-felt gratitude for direct and indirect support, love, care, friendship and laughter through many a dark night and ReDecision.

2nd Edition Workbook Completion

🙵 To Orbit Design for a beautiful new cover.

🙵 To Kim Dushinski and Tami DePalma at MarketAbility book publicity firm for use of computers/programs, time, tips, guidance andconstant support.

🙵 To Jeff Richards for a valuable answer on scanning.

🙵 And, to Brad Jorgensen for helping me reproof the text—one more last time!

Thank you all.

Though you cannot go back
and make a brand new start, my
friend, anyone can
start from now and
make a brand new end.

Unknown

Table of Contents

PART VIII: RESOURCES

Preface

I've not always been quite sure how I got where I am today, except that I have learned to trust myself and follow my vision and heart's desire thoroughly. In doing so I continue to realize *how much more* I have to learn to trust myself and follow my vision and heart's desire thoroughly.

Time and age have helped me to have a greater view and clearer hindsight of my journey to "here" from "there." My *job* in life has always been to help people. How I've done this has taken many forms. As I moved through social work jobs in mental health, adult rehabilitation, child psychiatric wards, chemical dependency and eating disorders, I felt discontent and frustrated most of the time. What I liked most was to teach, to educate others how to live life more fully. What I felt I was doing was pushing paper and fighting administration on poverty wages. My passion has been to assist others to live life less stressed and with more focus, consciousness and joy; to encourage them to risk, to go beyond their limits, old beliefs, conditioned and programmed life dramas; to stop making and using excuses, to stop blaming others or circumstance for their life situation and ultimately to *live their lives on purpose*—to get on with it before it's too late.

This mindset has led me to risk, experiment and dabble with many of my dreams and desires. I have done stand-up comedy, cut a music album as a song writer and singer and continued to discover, develop and unfold into my current work as a speaker, trainer, consultant and, now, author. Though my road map has always somehow seemed to make sense (to me) it has not been easy and I have not been lucky, as some people might think. As I've traveled steadily and persistently, my chosen route has been fraught with stop signs, detours, bridges out, closed roads, unhealthy and unkind passengers and travel companions and many other miscellaneous fears and disappointments.

TOOLS FOR THE JOURNEY

Our journey is always our own. What tools we choose, create and utilize are always individual decisions. My creative spirit has saved me along the miles. As a child, my mom did not especially see my spirit and determination as "creative"; she would scold me for being "stubborn" and wonder why I had to "know everything." We can laugh about it now, she's very aware how far my stubbornness, curiosity and love to "know everything" has taken me!

I have found, learned and developed several traveling tools that are constantly forming, growing and sharpening for my greatest use. These tools include my ability to let go and detach from others' judgments, rejection, opinions of me and my choices and sometimes from the people, places and things themselves that stop me from traveling my road. How long it takes me to let go is different for each issue that I experience. Sometimes I shift gears quickly, sometimes very slowly like everyone else can. I get hooked and caught up in the drama. Choosing to be aware and conscious as much as I can at all times and asking questions of myself and others helps to keep me flexible. Challenging ideals and mindsets that don't work or make sense lends itself to fewer self- and other-made blocks, to a life that rolls and weaves more easily with its natural ebb and flow.

One of my greatest gifts is to see humor in everything, especially myself (with a laugh that tends to embarrass people who are with me!). I once went to a psychic who said that in my most recent past life I was an Indian woman who was chosen to be the spokesperson for my tribe due to my ability to speak, negotiate, communicate and, moreover, to see everything lightly. She said that I have carried this same sense of leadership and humor into this life. She also said that I had an interesting name, it was Laughing Water. I asked, "Are you sure it wasn't Babbling Brook?"

The ability to laugh at the world and my life in it no matter what's happening—what my bank account looks like (*red* is a pretty color), how my body feels or looks (I don't own a scale), how my career is going (does *fired* mean anything to you?), and so on—has been my ticket to sanity. We all have *stuff* in our lives. That's life!

This book has come out of all these years and accumulated life lessons. It has been compiled and realized while dealing with three hospitalizations, five surgeries, constant rebalancing of medication for the past two years, a weight gain of 30 pounds due to the wrong medication and over seven years of chronic "female" pain and on and off depression. My life story to date is not unique. How each of us deals with our life's trials and experiences, however, is unique and the point of life itself—and this book.

PROCESS TIME

I had a lot of time to be quiet and think during my health crisis. It was a stopping point—a needed transition time for me. As I reexamined my life and work, I asked myself, "What is it that I do in my work with people?" I thought, "Well, I help people *decide* things." As I mulled this over and over, it came to me. I don't help people decide anything. If you're alive, you've decided a lot in life, or you wouldn't be here. I help people *RE-decide.* I help people make effective *redecisions* about the decisions and choices they've already made, consciously or unconsciously, that no longer work. "Oh!" Got it. And so was born the new name of my business, *ReDecisions Institute.*

LIGHTS ON THE PATH

This idea truly blossomed when, during this introspective time, I read Thomas Moore's book, *Care of the Soul.* When I read anything, I underline, write in the margins and put a lot of exclamation points and little faces on the pages. (My friends like borrowing my books, much faster reading when you know where all the good stuff is!) My copy of *Care of the Soul* is almost completely underlined, has tons of exclamation points, stars, check marks, faces and two rounded arrows (like the ones you'll see as The ReDecisions Model in this book) in the margins. Though this period of time has been frustrating and painful, filled with despair, fear, doubt and several suicidal thoughts of "life is meaningless," (isn't medication wonderful?!), my time in what is called the "dark night of the soul" or "underworld" experience was needed. I needed to stop, quiet down long enough to reexamine the puzzle pieces of my life, redecide where they fit and see a new and bigger picture of where I am, have been and am going. It's like I've pressed a "reset button" of who I am and what I am to be doing.

LETTING GO WITH ALL YOUR MIGHT

Though everything in this book is what I speak about and teach and think and live, constantly, the formulation of it into *Letting Go With All Your Might* "came out of nowhere." It has been a personal battle to write and to finish. Speaking comes naturally to me. It is fun and absolutely who I am. Writing this book has been a test in trusting myself to put my thoughts and words on paper. It hasn't flowed as easily as speaking. I don't have all those faces, nods and expressions to clue me in when my audience is understanding or not. It's new, it's unfamiliar and not as easy as I'd like.

After my brother Dave, a copywriter, reviewed the first draft of this book, he called me to ask if it was a thesis paper for college. The title at that time, *ReDecisions for Life: Living Between the Paradigms,* came from a weekend-intensive workshop I've offered. He said that it was too complicated and confusing—I had to "let go" of the first title, too. He wondered why I had included in the text numerous heavy, long supporting quotes and readings from other authors and books. He explained that I didn't have to prove myself, that I could trust myself to say what I wanted without all that

You will have wonderful surges forward. Then there must be a time of consolidating before the next forward surge.
Accept this as part of the process and never become downhearted.

Eileen Caddy
God Spoke to Me

Nothing bad ever happens to writers — everything is material.

Garrison Keillor
A Prairie Home Companion

backup, that my writing was fine.

Whew! Yes, trusting myself. Probably our greatest lesson. To *let go with all our might* and trust that we do know, that we can do it, that it will work, that it's okay. That we're okay.

So another step up on the evolutionary ladder, Life Lesson #506: Trusting Myself. The reward? A new identity, a new way to see myself and the world from this level. By the way, it's much better up here! I've also re-decided that if I have to literally "live" through my books, speaking topics and writing materials, then I'm going to take charge of my next project. My next book will be on tall men who wear cowboy boots and jeans who are really fun to be with and who enjoy me and life fully!

Growth always involves letting go of one thing to gain another. There is always a loss. This process for me has been to experience transition, endings and beginnings, the life/death/life cycle. I've let go of, cleaned out and let die many psychological, ego and fear driven parts of myself, again. I know there will be more that will come up to work on. That's a good thing. It means I'm alive.

THIS BOOK

This book is a simple yet serious look at this process of letting go. It follows and identifies the natural ebb and flow of life as we deal with times of change, transition, pain, loss, depression and grief of any kind. We each have the resources, options and opportunities to heal, change and choose responses and solutions for positive transformation and growth. The resources and options may not be readily apparent, but they are always right here. (This is the trust part.)

This process of change and transition has another side, too. When we "get" the Life Lesson, when we shift and redecide, we can feel more alive, excited, encouraged, open, new and renewed. There is no light without dark. And, hallelujah!, there is no dark without light! We can't have one side of the life process without the other.

TOUCHSTONE:
Life is very short. Enjoy it, experience it, feel it, laugh and cry it, live and die it.

Teaching people how to *see* life and events differently, to risk to change and grow, to let go and "get it" and to move up and on in their lives is my excitement and joy, it is my life's purpose. Living life fully offers each of us the opportunity to say that we are *living our purpose*, that we'll have fewer regrets when it's all said and done.

I hope that this book is helpful to you as you deal with life transitions, change, choices and making effective redecisions. To get you rolling, the following *Rules for Being Human* are a simply wonderful, true, yet tongue in cheek way to remind ourselves what this whole human experience thing is about. I hope they are useful.

The original author for the following rules is unknown. I have adapted them from a version by Dan Millman, author of *Way Of The Peaceful Warrior*.

THE RULES FOR BEING HUMAN

When you were born, you didn't come with an owner's manual; you have had to learn the rules the hard way. The following rules are intended to help you *lighten up* and make your life easier.

1. **You will receive a body.**
   Your body is your Earth suit. You may like it or hate it, but it will be yours for the entire period this time around. You have chosen its shape on a deeper level; leave it be or change it. Either way, love it.

2. **You will learn lessons.**
   You are enrolled in a full-time informal school called Life On Planet Earth. Each day in this school you will have the opportunity to learn lessons. You may like the lessons, hate them or think them irrelevant. You may learn them at your own pace, but you can only be expelled or leave once.

3. **There is no failure and no mistakes, only lessons.**
   Growth is a process of experimentation—trial and error. The so-called failed experiments are as much a part of the process as the experiment that ultimately "works." Learn from everything and everyone.

4. **You will have classmates, teachers and students.**
   You will have a choice of who is in your life and why. All people are your teachers. Some will be your students and still others will be enjoyable classmates for play and fun. Make clear choices about how and when others are in your life. Most people spend far too many years in drama class. Others are merely mirrors of and for you. You cannot love or hate something about another person unless it reflects to you

Life is what you make it.

Victor Frankl

something you love or hate in yourself; that you are running away from or striving for; fear or desire.

5. **A lesson is repeated until learned.**
    A lesson will be presented to you in various forms until you have learned it. When you've learned it, you can then go on to the next lesson. If you don't learn easy lessons, they become harder. You will know you've learned a lesson when your mindset and actions change.

6. **Learning lessons does not end.**
    There is no part of life that does not contain its lessons. Every person, every incident is the universal teacher. If you are alive, there are lessons to be learned.

7. **"There" is no better than "here."**
    Nothing leads to happiness. When you're "there" has become a "here," you will simply obtain another "there" that again looks better than "here."

8. **What you learn in Life On Planet Earth—what you create of your life—is up to you.**
    There are three kinds of people,
    >   those who make things happen,
    >   those who watch what happens, and
    >   those who wonder what happened.

    Life is like a movie; you may feel like a bit player, but you have the power to become screen writer, casting director, choreographer, producer and director. It's your movie. You have all the tools and resources you need; what you do with them is up to you. Notice that you do have the courage to take the necessary risks and that fear is normal; take charge of your life. If you don't someone else will.

9. **Your answers lie inside you.**
    All you need to do is to look, listen and trust. Then you'll realize that you are the spiritual being you've been seeking.

10. **You will tend to forget all this.**

— Denver, Colorado
November 1994

It is never too late—
in fiction or in life
to revise.

Nancy Thayer

Welcome to my 2ⁿᵈ Edition Workbook of *Letting Go With All Your Might*

Yes, every now and then, we must revise! It has been seven long years since this book and I had to "let go with all our might", and nine years since I let go of more than I can believe. Long painful stories of experiencing physical changes and emotional challenges through too many surgeries, moving from Colorado twice and back again, losing the flourishing speaking career I once had due to changes in markets (can you say "Healthcare Reform?") and so income, and sobbing for days and weeks at a time wondering how to pull it all together again.

Feeling lost many times in longing and struggle to hold onto my visions and ideals is not a new story, but it was mine for awhile. From mid-life crisis to mid-life "adventure", as tides and cycles go, they do turn. I am back, finding and creating new and wonderful ways to offer my gifts and talents again.

Thank God for good friends, inspirational writings, the technology to support my ongoing dreams and visions—and the ability to trust that the law of nature and cycles does work to support the change we desire.

— Longmont, Colorado
April 2002

Often, in order to stay alive, we have to unmake a living in order to get back to living the life we wanted for ourselves. It is the cycle of making, disintegration and remaking that is the hallmark of meaningful and creative work.

David Whyte
Crossing the Unknown Sea: Work as a Pilgrimage of Identity

I

---·•●•·---

Letting Go
With All Your Might

---·•●•·---

Ultimately, we need to let go of
preconceptions about our world.
We have no obligation to be who we were;
nor should we pressure others to meet our expectations.
Expect the unexpected; be ready for surprises!
Nothing is fixed; the world is different from moment to
moment.

Ken Bear Hawk
Creation Spirituality Magazine

*People like us, who believe in physics,
know that the distinction between past, present, and future
is only a stubbornly persistent illusion.*

Albert Einstein

Chapter 1

LETTING GO

*The greatest discovery of my generation
is that human beings,
by changing their inner attitudes of their minds,
can change the outer aspects of their lives.*

William James
(1842-1910)

Life is a struggle — because of attachment. We hold on to people, places, things and ideals. We have expectations, judgments, rules and fears that we use to try to control others and the outside world, and that ultimately control us.

We watch ourselves and others attach and hold on every day. Children learn attachment and mistrust early in life. A child asks you to fix a broken toy, yet won't *let go* of it so that you can fix it. We see this same behavior in animals. To capture monkeys in the jungle is quite easy. Put bananas in the hole of a tree; the monkey reaches in for the fruit, gathers up a fist full and can't pull its hand back out. To let go of the fruit means freedom, to hold on to the fruit means capture—control by others. What are you holding onto that keeps you imprisoned?

"Just let go!" It sounds so easy. To let go means to trust in yourself, others and the process.

In one of my workshops on forgiveness and trusting again after divorce, a woman became enraged at the thought of trusting her former husband. In so many words she said, "I could never trust him again. He's a jerk and a turkey!" I suggested that she trust that he'll always be a jerk and a turkey. She stopped, stared at me and calmed down within seconds. With a grin, she replied, "Oh! I can do that."

Like the woman from my workshop, we all find reasons to hold on to anger, resentment, blame, fear and other emotions and memories that cause us pain. Holding on creates an illusion of control and power, but it also creates frustration, bitterness and increased pain.

The Cycle of Attachment is illustrated as follows:

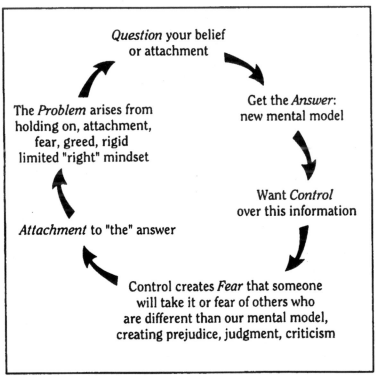

Figure 1: Cycle of Attachment

*To be free
we must be comfortable
in being someone,
anyone or no one
at anytime in any place.
Attachment is
our greatest self-cruelty.*

Sujata
Beginning to See

The hook lies in the illusion that we need to know everything and then own it, control it. The truth is, it's wonderful to know and to experience everything we can in life and to let these experiences weave in and out of us, making us richer for it. Letting go means to enjoy, learn and experience life without attaching.

TOUCHSTONE:
When we attach to anything, we are controlled by it.

So, if letting go is the answer, the question is: What are we letting go of? We let go of conditioned, patterned beliefs, our ego—anything and anyone that holds us back, squelches our spirit and limits our ability to live fully and wholly (holy). By *detaching*, letting go, we free ourselves and others to live life fully. Below is a list of areas in life we hold on to. Being aware of these areas can help us let go.

relationships	false pride	knowing the answers
youth	plans	grief
age	anger	loss
money	expectations	gain
titles	death	holding on to
labels	life itself	owning
power	fear	security
memories	despair	significance
goals	love	importance
control	hate	tradition
needs	pain	being right
wants	joy	perfectionism
beliefs	denial	achievement
dreams	habit	winning
thoughts	patterns	certainty
desires	judgment	health
wishes	criticism	blame
failure	righteousness	arrogance
success	truth	"the way it should/ought to be"
guilt	facts	"the way it must be/has to be"
shame	resentment	"the way it's always been"
paranoia	bitterness	"the way it can't be"
mistrust	loyalties	"the way it is"
comfort	happiness	illusions

There is only one courage and that is the courage to go on dying to the past, not to collect it, not to accumulate it, not to cling to it. We all cling to the past, and because we cling to the past we become unavailable to the present.

Bhagwan Shree Rajneesh
*Walking in Zen,
Sitting in Zen*

LIFE PROCESS

To live life fully, and to feel more connected to ourselves and the world, we must let go to the process. What is the process? The *process* is the ebb and flow of the life/death/life cycle. This is the natural cycle of life that is made up of continuous endings and beginnings.

Throughout life we have ongoing opportunities, or Life Lessons, that challenge us to hold on or let go, block or change, stagnate or flow, attach or detach. This cycle of life is never ending, drawing us up through the spiral of life, inviting us to grow and change.

Whenever there is a "this," there will be a "that." When you obtain "that" and it becomes "this," there will be a "that" again. We attach and detach, hold on and let go daily—this is normal and natural. The dilemma is created when we don't want to let go and it is time, and often past time, to do so.

TOUCHSTONE:
To get THERE from HERE we have to let go of something. To get THAT when we have THIS we have to let go.

Be patient toward all that is unsolved in your heart and learn to love the questions themselves, like locked rooms and like books that are written in a very foreign tongue. Do not seek the answers, which cannot be given you because you would not be able to live them.

Rainer Maria Rilke

We can find ourselves saying, "But I'm *trying* to let go. I'm *trying* to change." We are putting all of the mindful energy and thoughtful action into the situation drawing us to change, but it just doesn't seem to be happening. I've heard many times that you can't *try* to do anything. You either do it or not, but there is no try. I disagree. Life is art—it is ever changing and challenging us to develop and grow. There are times we can judge those who say they are trying and we know they are not. Other times, we truly are doing everything we know to change and move on. There is a natural time of incubation, when answers percolating deep inside are waiting to come up and out when they're ready. And the "timing of the universe" isn't usually the same as our own.

These times of trial and inner battles can feel frustrating, lonely and dark. To reemerge from times of confusion and even hopelessness into the light of feeling in control again takes much trust, faith and inner work. It takes *letting go with all your might.*

BANK ON CHANGE

As with the life/death/life cycle, all things are constantly transforming and will eventually die. Life is about letting go of our impossible craving for certainty or significance; letting go of our demands on the universe for perfect happiness and everlasting life. Our only option may be to learn the wisdom of insecurity and a way to be comfortable with unfamiliarity. To accept uncertainty as our philosophy might allow us to honor each other more, show tolerance for one another more and for those who speak truths we don't wish to hear—delighting in all the bizarre and wondrous interpretations of the mystery, life.[1]

THIS BOOK

This book teaches the reader the simple message of learning how to come home to oneself—to live a life of a human "being" instead of a human "doing." We can choose to minimize our frustrations and struggles by not taking ourselves quite so seriously—by learning to see life *hugely* and to laugh, a lot.

Each time you let go, release your hold, you create thresholds, doorways of change. This book is about letting go of attachments. It is a guide to choice, change and making effective redecisions for life. Through an 11-Stage ReDecisions Model, stories and quotes, I will explain how to let go of limiting conditioned beliefs, patterned conditioning and other conscious and unconscious limits.

The central message in *Letting Go With All Your Might* is that, though life can seem very hard at times, learning to flow with the cycles of life, weaving in and out of life transitions and consciously experiencing life, ultimately creates personal fulfillment and experience beyond expectation.

In this book, we will explore the following:

❧ *Beliefs*, values and perceptions and how we can get stuck in them

❧ *Transitions*—how they work, how to understand them and how to have more control over them and their toll on our control issues, our ego and our identity

❧ *Confusion, Fear and Doubt* we can feel in dealing with change and letting go of beliefs and the struggle and despair we can feel in our journey through what is called the "dark night of the soul"

❧ *Surrender and Trust* in a life/death/life cycle that prunes us up for a better life experience

❧ *Passages*—where we let go and ready ourselves for new awareness

❧ *Acceptance and Hope* for new direction and answers to our confusion and fear

❧ *The Black Hole*—where we attach, hold on, fight change and struggle against surrender, trust and letting go

❧ *Mental Model Shifts and ReDecisions*—where we "get it" and move on to our new awareness, identity and "new normal"

I trust you've been to each of these places. I certainly have. Fortunately or unfortunately, I also know that you will be in each of these places again, and so will I.

Too many humans have developed knowledge without wisdom, skill without heart, left brain without right, yang without yin. We know how to do but not how to be.

Wes "Scoop" Nisker
Crazy Wisdom

Approach it and there is no beginning; follow it and there is no end. You can't know it, but you can be it, at ease in your own life.

Lao Tzu

This book is not therapy but an educational guide. It is about choice—your choice to change, from the inside out. Your choice to be, do and have what it is you dream of. Your choice to cut down on accumulating regrets. Your choice to live life fully and consciously.

STOP. SIT. BREATHE. AND DO THE WORK

Throughout this book you will have the opportunity to work on letting go through exercises in each chapter. Though I've left much space to make notes throughout these pages, I invite you to have a notebook available and to take the time to work through them. There are stories to illustrate experiences of change and transition, and many supportive and introspective quotes that expand my ideas. Wherever possible I have included extra information with each quote: the reference source of the quote, and information about its author. The Bibliography section of this book follows up on other reference sources as well. In the Resource section are suggested books and movies for expanded awareness and learning regarding letting go and the redecisions process.

Throughout the chapters you will find *Touchstones*—little night-lights, one-line reminders, thoughts and ideas of how the world works and how to better learn to work with it.

My goal is to help you:

- ❧ Identify your conditioned belief systems.
- ❧ Question beliefs that do not serve you.
- ❧ Let go of old, limiting beliefs, choices and mindsets.
- ❧ Identify attachments and limited perceptions.
- ❧ Be flexible during times of change and transition.
- ❧ Deal with and understand the dark and hard times, empty feelings and frustrating times.
- ❧ Recognize "wake-up calls" and other life lessons for growth.
- ❧ Understand growth and healing, the natural life process, through life/death/life cycles.
- ❧ Deal with the struggle of being caught between mental models.
- ❧ Recognize your control and responsibility over life's endings and beginnings.
- ❧ Take control of your beliefs, consciously redecide and proactively respond.

Don't try to force anything.
Let life be a deep let-go.
See God opening millions of
flowers every day
without forcing the buds.

Bhagwan Shree Rajneesh
Dying for Enlightenment

Gain these tools and methods to help create a more aligned and flowing life more open and acknowledging of joy, purpose and creativity no matter what is happening around you.

ReDeciding for life is not about striving for perfection, but about moving beyond and away from fear, limits and regrets into wholeness and life. Your growth and newness is the reward for your work. Trust your trials, frustrations and sometimes, deep suffering as the seeds of an awakening.

TOUCHSTONE:
You're not here for a long time, you're here for a good time.

*Those who want to follow
the Way of Beauty
must break away from
cultural dictatorship
and move out into a
no-man's land where
everything is new and unknown.
They must learn to live outside
the stereotypes and
worn-out attitudes,
and free themselves from any
bonds—roles, ties, ideologies,
interests, or habits—that might
hold them back.
They must learn all over again,
without fear or hesitation,
to be themselves.*

Piero Ferruci
Inevitable Grace

> *Finding your own path of power*
> *[a way of working and using all your energy]*
> *is not always easy.*
> *For me to do it, I had to tear up both the white man's*
> *and the Indian's scripts for life.*
> *If you wish to walk the path of power,*
> *you must do the same.*
>
> Sun Bear

Chapter 2

REDECISIONS FOR LIFE

❧

The question is not,
"What if I die tomorrow?"
It is
*"What if I live another 20 or 30
years the way I am?"*

Kim Wolinski

❧

❧ Would you like to be happier? More relaxed? Less stressed?

❧ Would you like to take more risks? Strive for specific goals?

❧ Would you like to feel healthier? Manage your time and energy better?

❧ Would you like to have fewer regrets? Enjoy your life more?

Of course. And you can. So, what is keeping you from these experiences? The answer—beliefs.

BELIEFS

There is nothing to prevent you from being, doing and having what you can imagine for yourself, except for the limitations of your beliefs about yourself.

As a man thinks, so he is.

Proverbs

Beliefs are our truth. Beliefs are what we unquestioningly think is true about ourselves and the world, according to what we learned from others, especially in our formative years. Beliefs are created through the conditioning we are exposed to on an ongoing basis by parents, family, teachers, religion, cultural-ethnic backgrounds, politics, the media and society in general. We've come to accept our beliefs for the most part unconsciously, as the truth, the way it is, and moreover, the way it will always be.

TOUCHSTONE:
If you believe something long enough, you become it.

MENTAL MODELS

Our beliefs are a way of "seeing" and "knowing" things in our lives. They form a mentel model known as the "hypnosis of social conditioning." "Mental models" are deeply engrained assumptions, generalizations, or even pictures or images that influence how we understand the world and how we take action. Very often, we are not consciously aware of our mental models or the effects that they have on our behavior.[2] They are the conditioned information we take in during a lifetime and become the filters through which we view everything and everyone. For example, you see someone dressed elegantly and may assume he is wealthy and intelligent. You see someone who is unkempt and mismatched and may think that he is unintelligent, careless and low income.

We not only have mental models—thoughts, assumptions and mindsets—about everyone and everything we see and experience, but we have feelings about them, too. We can feel comfortable and open to people who are like us and afraid and defensive to those who are not. We treat people differently who we think are different than we are, we invite those into our lives and share opportunities more easily with those with whom we relate.

Mental models are learned assumptions and ways of thinking. To break past these conditioned ways of thinking takes inner, personal work. As adults, we can choose to be aware of our prejudices, judgments and criticisms that "box" people, places, things and experiences into our safe and secure, usually unconscious, categories of thinking and seeing. By being aware of these mindsets, we can also make the effort to change them, and so, change ourselves.

In order to let go of what doesn't work and to gain our new reality, our new truths, we must become conscious of our life/work patterns and conditioned beliefs. To create your life differently—happier, more relaxed, less stressful, healthier, wealthier—you must examine the don't work and could be different. Our beliefs become false, old and

Take a day to heal from the lies you've told yourself and that have been told to you.

Maya Angelou

assumptions you inherited about who you are and consciously redefine the true nature of yourself and your life.

TOUCHSTONE:
We each live, work, play and create by a set of beliefs that we hold as the truth, the way it is, the way it should be.

Many of the beliefs we live by are not true.

Have you ever questioned your beliefs? How did it feel? Sometimes questioning "carved in stone" traditional or familiar thinking, doing and being can feel like a betrayal of someone else or of ourselves. It's uncomfortable, unfamiliar territory. The unknown. It may, in fact, have felt so uncomfortable that you ended up with a "terminal disease of certainty" or a "hardening of the categories."[3]

We tend to see, and to like, life and things in "boxes" and "categories." Defining life this way does help us to know who we are, where we belong in families, cultures, organizations and such. It helps to explain the world to us and helps us to predict its behavior. Defining life this way can also hold us in boxed mindsets. A mindset that is limited to only a few definitions of self and life offers one little movement in the world of creativity, freedom and the joy of living.

TOUCHSTONE:
Conditioned beliefs are limiting because they render us blind to alternatives.

You might also identify times when you have questioned your beliefs, worked to change your mindset about something that was not working for you, and found it to be a wonderful experience. Moving past old habits, old truths and conditioned beliefs open up opportunities in our worlds we may have never seen before. We may realize the opportunities were there all along—we just didn't have the eyes to see them.

Our beliefs of "the truth" changes. They change as we change. They are shown to be incorrect by new information and key questions. By observing others, and their life choices and process, we notice differences and begin to see and to know that some things in our lives

*At first people refuse to believe
that a strange new thing
can be done,
then they begin to hope
it can be done,
then they see it can be done—
then it is done and all the world
wonders why it was not done
centuries ago.*

Frances Hodgson Burnett

don't work and could be different. Our beliefs become false, old an outdated when time, science, technology or personal experience show reason to review, redefine and redecide them and their evolution.

In the 15 years that I have worked with others as a therapist, educator, speaker and friend, I have watched with great fascination and joy the redecisions others have made when they could see that their beliefs were false or at least a bit off center. The core of what I teach asks the following: *"Are you living your life's purpose? If not, why not? And what are you going to do about it?"* It's hard to live your purpose (what you're here to *be* and *do* in your lifetime) when conditioned beliefs keep you stuck.

TOUCHSTONE:
We never stop changing as long as we're alive.

THE OAK AND THE WILLOW

Nature is a great storyteller, giving many examples and analogies of our human world. The difference between the oak tree and the weeping willow as they relate to our beliefs and mindsets is one of these. At the core of any belief lies the conviction that there is no other choice, that "this" (whatever "this" is at the time) is the only way, and "this" is the truth. Like an oak tree, conditioned beliefs and rigid mindsets are solid—they don't bend. And, like an oak tree in a storm, conditioned beliefs will stand firm, struggle and fight against times of questioning and need for change—and break. On the other hand, open-minded mindsets are like willow trees—flexible. When storms blow, they bend and flow in the wind. There is less or little struggle and fighting against what is happening as focus and direction change. The paradox, then, is that to bend, to examine our beliefs, to let go and to be willing to change, requires much strength.

TOUCHSTONE:
Redecisions and change can come the hard way, or they can be made much easier with our conscious help in the process.

Can you change your mind about what you believe to be true? Being open to alternatives is always an option. Happy, healthy people live by being flexible to change. Being flexible to change means being willing to ask yourself questions that challenge your belief system, your mental models and your very self

TOUCHSTONE:
Change is inevitable. Growth is optional.

FAMILY RECIPE

Here is a well-worn story that illustrates our inability to see simple decisions and choices that are ripe for evaluation and change. There was a college student, we'll call her Alice, who visited her parents for Thanksgiving. She had brought her friend, Jamie, who helped her with the family dinner. As Jamie watched, Alice prepared the ham by slicing off both ends, adding a couple of slices of pineapple on the top and finishing it off with a few red shiny cherries held in by toothpicks. Jamie asked Alice why she cut off both ends of the ham. Was it a family recipe, did it cook faster, did it baste itself? Alice explained that was the way her mother always did it and they should ask her.

Upon asking Alice's mother, Carol, why they cut off both ends of the ham before cooking it, Carol said, "I don't know. My mother taught me how to cook, and that's the way she always did it. Let's ask grandma." They called Martha into the kitchen and asked her the same question. Martha had the same response, "I don't know. My mother taught me how to cook, and that's the way she did it." Well, great-grandma Mildred was there for the Thanksgiving feast, so they called her into the kitchen. The women asked her why they cut off both ends of the ham before cooking it. Mildred slowly eyed the ham on the cabinet, then responded, "When I was young, I grew up on a farm. We butchered our own meat. If you didn't cut off both ends of the ham, you couldn't get it into the pan. Now, I don't know why *you're* doing that. This ham is pretty small already, you'd better put those ends back on."

REDECISIONS

Letting go and redeciding provides the opportunity to rethink any situation and life choice. Doing the work of rethinking and redeciding, uncovers, discovers and creates options that enhance and support our life at its very core, and often, our life purpose.

Why is this information important? Scientific, medical and psychological research show that when we are more aware, take more control over our lives, thoughts and choices, and adapt more easily to the ebb and flow of life, we have less negative stress, better mental health and, overall, better physical health. To enjoy life is a personal responsibility, attainable through shifting our mindset—making conscious redecisions for life.

*If we would only give,
just once,
the same amount of reflection to
what we want to get out of life
that we give to the question of
what to do with a
two week vacation,
we would be startled at our false
standards and the aimless
procession of our busy days.*

Dorothy Canfield Fisher
American author
and essayist
(1879-1958)

EXERCISE:
Different people and cultures have particular and often creative ways of reevaluating one's life process. When Indigenous People are having problems, feeling ill or frustrated with life, they ask the following four questions.[4] Take time to answer them for yourself.

1. **When in your life did you stop singing?**
   Where you stopped singing is where you stopped trusting yourself; where you began to lose your soul, where you lost your voice, your own truth.

2. **When did you stop dancing?**
   When did you begin to lose touch with your body?

   Stay connected to your *four bones.*
   a. Your backbone: courage
   b. Your funny bone: sense of humor, which keeps you flexible
   c. Your wishbone: your dreams, vision, wishes and hopes
   d. Your hollow little bone: the hollow little bone is connected to the body bringing all of life through it to you and your body. Let the mystery work and come *through* you instead of you trying to work it. Be more spontaneous.

3. **When did you stop being enchanted with stories and particularly your own life story?**
   Stories are the greatest healing, teaching art that we have, transmitting values, ethics, tradition and memories. Think about your favorite childhood stories. What are the life stories you like to hear? What stories do you tell and share?

4. **When did you stop being comfortable with the sweet territory of silence?**
   Silence is that place where we can contemplate and reflect in our own solitude. This place of quiet nurtures the soul, giving us the opportunity to listen to our own nature within, where we learn to trust ourselves.

Shifting our mindset asks us to live a life of healthy or "divine" discontent. Creating your life by your deepest interests and values is to endlessly question your understanding of yourself and the world, your beliefs, values and identity. This conscious process of cleaning out, learning and expanding who we are is the movement

You will decide on a matter, and it will be established for you, and light will shine on your wings.

Job 22:28
The Bible

May you discover the path leading to that best and truest portion of yourself.

Rianne La Cross
Greeting Card

from what is called the "false self," that conditioned and programmed self of who we are, into the "true Self," that more conscious, honest, whole (and holy) person we are *always* in the process of "becoming."

EXERCISE:
Create two columns on a sheet of paper. Title the left column: INTERESTS; the right column: VALUES. Make time to be quiet and reflect on these two issues. Write down your deepest INTERESTS. What INTERESTS you in the world? Then write down your deepest VALUES. What do you VALUE most in life?

As you write these two lists, you may find some overlap. It's okay to have some of the same items in each. After you've finished your lists, take time to reflect on what you have written. Your INTERESTS and VALUES include your inner longings, desires, creative forces and highest avenues of fulfillment. Use these lists to set goals—they will always bring you home to your truest self.

Take charge of your life, present and future. Give yourself focus and direction.

TOUCHSTONE:
If you don't know who you are and what you want—who does?

*I've just changed
my whole value system;
I know what's important.
I want to be a good dad,
I want to be a good husband.
That's my top priority.
And if I can still do my work,
well, great.*

Rocker Bob Seger, 49,
on getting off the road

II

Mental Models
and Their Shifts

Change - real change - comes from the inside out.
It doesn't come from
hacking at the leaves of attitude and behavior
with quick fix personality ethic techniques.
It comes from striking at the root - the fabric of our thought,
the fundamental, essential paradigms which
give definition to our character and
create the lens through which we see the world.

Stephen Covey
The Seven Habits of Highly Effective People

You should not let all expectation of good be worn away.
Nothing painless the all-accomplishing King dispenses
for mortal man; but grief and joy come circling to all,
like the turning paths of the Bear among the stars.
The shimmering night does not stay for men,
nor does calamity, nor wealth.
But swiftly they are gone,
and for another man it comes—to know joy and its loss.

Sophocles

Chapter 3

MENTAL MODEL

We do not see things as they are.
We see them as we are.

The Talmud

As defined earlier, "mental models" are deeply ingrained assumptions, generalizations, or even pictures or images that influence how we understand the world and how we take action. Very often, we are not consciously aware of our mental models or the effects that they have on our behavior.[5]

In the corporate world the term *paradigm* has been used for some time to explain mental models. Paradigm is pronounced "pair a dime" and it comes from the Greek *paradeigma,* which means "pattern." When we are in a paradigm, or mental model, it is hard to imagine any other way of thinking. We're right. This or that is the way it is—period.

Our mental models tend to exist unquestioned. They are transmitted through culture and to succeeding generations through direct experience rather than being taught.[6] "This is the way we've *always* done it." (Doesn't *everyone*?) "This is the way it's always been."

Your mental model is your belief system, your entire conscious and unconscious perceptual system. Whether right or wrong, desirable or undesirable, new or outdated, healthy or destructive, limiting or of reality.

TOUCHSTONE:
Sometimes we're wrong.

SHIFTING

What does it mean to *shift* a mental model? When you *shift* your mental model, you let go of the belief, model, ideal, example, vision of reality, pattern or framework of thought that does not work or serve you. It is literally "shifting" out of the mindset where you've been to a new belief, view or ideal...to a new mental model.

My two definitions of a shift:
1. "Oh!"
2. "Aha!"

Like the light switch, it must occur all at once. New mental models are not figured out, but suddenly *seen* and *felt*.[7] Do you remember the last time you had or felt an "Oh!" or an "Aha!", when every cell in your body "got it"? You became aware of a new way of seeing, understanding or thinking about something. It may have been your experience of learning a new language, a sport activity, a skill or a new way to communicate and relate to another person, place, thing or idea. Your belief changed about the subject from the way you used to think about it or see it (your old mental model) to this new understanding (your new mental model). It literally *shifted*. And whether you said it out loud or felt it like a "switch" in your mind or body, you thought, "Oh!" or "Aha!" "I get it!" That's it. That's a mental model shift.

TOUCHSTONE:
Mental models can keep us grounded and connected to our work, play, families, culture, life-style and dreams.

Mental models can keep us stuck, angry, depressed, limited, blocked and even ill.

Do not seek illumination unless you seek it as a man whose hair is on fire seeks a pond.

Sri Rmakrishna

LIVING BETWEEN PARADIGMS AND MENTAL MODELS

We live our lives between mental models, constantly modifying our beliefs or framework of thought in great and small changes and shifts. Sometimes we do this transitional process of change and letting go quite unconsciously; other times, consciously, with much deliberation and concentrated effort.

At times we kick and scream our way through and between the mental models. The premise of this book is to offer guidance through this process of shifting in order to move more consciously, more smoothly, sometimes more quickly, and ultimately more deeply, through the stages of mental model shifts, transition, and redecisions. Throughout this book I will interchange the words *belief*, *mental model*, *paradigm*, or *mindset*, meaning the same thing.

EXERCISE:
To identify the various mental models or paradigms you live in, and live out, complete the following sentences:

1. I live in this (area, city, state, country) because . . . .
2. What I do for a living is (occupation) because . . . .
3. I am in relationship with my spouse/partner because . . . .
4. The people who are my friends are my friends because . . . .
5. My parents are . . . because . . . .
6. My children are . . . because . . . .
7. The life-style I live is this way because . . . .
8. The religion I am a member of is . . . because . . . .
9. My political affiliation is . . . because . . . .
10. I am happy in life because . . . .
11. I am frustrated in life because . . . .
12. My health is . . . because . . . .
13. My financial situation is . . . because . . . .
14. My life is . . . because . . . .

How you complete each of these sentences is true for you, because you believe that they are true. How effectively we deal with change, transition and the process of endings and beginnings (letting go of the old and embracing the new) is dependent on the depth and loyalty we have to our mental models and our willingness to "shift" them.

The curious paradox is that when I accept myself just as I am, then I can change.

Carl Rogers
Pioneer in Psychotherapy

Humankind has two basic and equally strong needs:
stability and change.
The issue is not either/or;
it's creating a context in which
pursuing the novel is cherished.

Tom Peters

Chapter 4

CHANGE

A tiny change today
makes for a dramatically different tomorrow.

Richard Bach
ONE

How do you deal with change? Check one of the following:

_____1. I love change.
Change is a great thing. I love exploring and finding out
new things about myself and the world, new ways of
"seeing" everything.

_____ 2. I can deal with change pretty well.
I try new things occasionally. Sometimes it's
uncomfortable, but mostly it's okay.

_____ 3. I can flow all right with changes that happen, if I have to.
But I'd rather not if I don't have to. It's uncomfortable
for me.

_____ 4. Forget it.
I like things just the way they are, so don't bother me.

PERCEPTIONS OF CHANGE

The following are two ways to look at change.

POSITIVE ASPECTS OF CHANGE:	NEGATIVE ASPECTS OF CHANGE:
Joy	Fear
Excitement	Reluctance
Open minded	Closed minded
Open emotionally	Closed emotionally
Good	Bad
Desirable	Undesirable
Opportunity	Risky
Growth	Paralysis
Challenge	Letting go of safety/security
New choices	Changing the status quo
New direction	Uncomfortable
New found personal power	Dangerous
Tap untapped resources	Crisis
Creativity	Comfort zone challenged
Knowledge	Unknown
Wisdom	Not seen as necessary
Learn from the past	Repeat old beliefs/actions
Adventure	Familiarity
In control	Out of control
Act	React
Life	Death

*All things
are in the act of change;
thou thyself in ceaseless
transformation and
partial decay,
and the whole universe
with thee.*

Marcus Aurelius Antonius

EXERCISE:
Change. What does this word mean to you? Answer the following questions to see if you can gain more clarity regarding your beliefs about change:

1. Where did you learn about change?
2. What did you learn from your father about dealing with change?
3. What did you learn from your mother about dealing with change?
4. What does risk-taking mean to you?
5. How do you feel about taking risks?
6. Where did you learn about taking risks?
7. What did you learn from your father about risk-taking?
8. What did you learn from your mother about risk-taking?

Most likely, if you grew up in an environment that showed fear and
speaking? Public speaking is not hard—it can be learned. Apparently
it is fear-rendering in and of itself, although we all like to talk about

gnashing of teeth whenever anything called for a change in the ordinary, you may not be one of the century's all-time great change agents. We learn from our families, cultures and communities as we grow up how to fear change or how to embrace it.

Since most of the blocks and resistance to change comes from emotional and psychological fears learned early in life, it is important to look at these fears that can eventually become the blocks that keep us stuck. Three fears that teach us to limit our risk-taking tendencies and influence us from a very young age are learned from others around us.

1. Fear of abandonment
2. Fear of separation
3. Fear of rejection

ABANDONMENT

Fear starts early in our lives. Babies are born with only two natural fears: the fear of falling and the fear of loud noises.[8] Learning to fear abandonment comes quickly. Many adults do not experience the fear of abandonment. It is a natural growth adjustment from the helpless infant stage of life, where we needed someone to take care of us to survive. Unfortunately, due to intensely frightening experiences as children, some adults have ongoing issues of abandonment for a lifetime. Fearful childhood experiences can create feelings from mildly uncomfortable to deeply threatening anxieties of being left behind, alone, neglected and...abandoned.

SEPARATION

Fear of separation is learned in different ways. For example, a child who has not been prepared to be away from his routine and environment may find it overwhelming to go off to school for the first time.

Fear of separation can also come from religious teachings, such as the fear and guilt of sinning, being "separated" from God. Much neurotic guilt, shame and paranoia is created through unbalanced preaching of who God is and how God works in people's lives. If you sin and are then separated from God, there is a constant fear of doing anything that will "make God mad or unhappy" with you. Fear and paranoia do not support the creation of fertile ground for change, risk-taking and growth.

REJECTION

Did you know that the greatest cause of fear (marked above death and being burned alive on causes-of-fear questionnaires) is public

I have three phobias which, could I mute them, would make my life as slick as a sonnet, but as dull as ditch water: I hate to go to bed, I hate to get up, and I hate to be alone.

Tallulah Bankhead
American actress
(1903-1968)

speaking? Public speaking is not hard - it can be learned. Apparently it is fear-rendering in and of itself, although we all like to talk about ourselves and our interests. The fear of public speaking is really about *rejection.*

As a public speaker, you express your opinions and beliefs, style and skills in front of many others. A public speaker is a clear target for criticism, judgment and rejection. People may not like you, they may challenge you or laugh at you. You are naked, vulnerable to the world. I have many colleagues in the business of professional speaking. It's common to hear, "I got 1,000 great reviews and evaluations after the program. And then, there was that one...." Is it what someone said (their opinion) or is it your conditioned fear, triggered from past experience or beliefs?

I'd try to be my own best friend...
but I fear rejection!

Ziggy
Tom Wilson, cartoonist

TOUCHSTONE:
Not everyone is going to like you or your choices. That's okay.

I tend to use the following formula to decide how I'm doing and if I need to pursue a change based on others' feedback. It is something I heard many, many times when I worked in the chemical dependency field years ago. "If a lot of people in your life are telling you that you walk like a duck, talk like a duck and look like a duck—you might be a duck. It's time to listen, learn and change. But if only a few people tell you this, and everyone else says you're fine, you're probably fine."

CONTROL AND STRUGGLE

Many of us resist change and think of it as something that happens "to" us. Learned psychological fears and conditioned beliefs are a major influence in resisting change. We tend to wait to change until *not* changing becomes intolerable. So, consider what is happening between needing to change and finally changing—usually a mess.

Why do we struggle and fight against ourselves and wait so long to do what we already know we are to do? Being human is an interesting concept. Our free will gets us into many jams and ulcers due to "willfully" waiting, worrying, procrastinating, fighting, pushing, pulling, shoving and basically going out of our way not to change.

At a speaking engagement in Florida, I thought I'd have an adventure and swim with the dolphins. I'm not much of a water person (*JAWS* didn't help) so snorkeling lessons were in line. Pedro, a 68-year-old born-to-swim kind of guy, was my instructor at the hotel pool. We practiced snorkeling techniques there, then went out to the sea. He took my hand as we started to go out into the water. After a minute or two of "working at swimming out there," Pedro pulled my hand back and stopped me. He asked, "What are you doing?" I said, "I'm swimming out into the ocean." He said, "You don't have to *swim out* into the ocean, just flip your flippers a little, *it* will *take you out*." I rolled my eyes and said, "This is how I do most of life!"

RESISTANCE

Change. Is it desirable or undesirable? That, of course, depends on what the change is. For the most part, change is desirable. Change is the process through which we can explore, expand, transform, redevelop and recreate our lives. Even when change is painful or perceived as bad or undesirable, there are lessons that can give us great insight into who we are. Without embracing or surrendering to change, we miss the associated self-discovery.

The reasons we avoid change are numerous. Some of the most common are:

1. Fear of rejection.
   "What will they think of me?"
2. Fear of failure.
   "If I try, it might not work."
3. Fear of success.
   "If I succeed, what will they expect of me next?"
4. Denial.
   "I'm fine the way I am...but you *could change...."*
5. Negativism.
   "I can't, so why try?"
6. Habit.
   "I've always been this way."
7. Low self-esteem.
   "I'll never be worth much, no matter what I do or how much I change."
8. Fear of the unknown.
   "Who knows what might happen!"
9. Inconvenience.
   "I'd have to change my whole schedule."
10. Uncertainty over the reward.
    "Will it be worth it?"
11. Fear of looking silly or dumb.
    "Can you image what I'd look like? I don't want to make a fool of myself."
12. Threat to security.
    "Will they still like me if I do better than they do?"
13. Fear of confrontation: real or imagined opposition from others.
    "My spouse (parent, someone outside of self) would never

*Journeys bring
power and love back into you.
If you can't go somewhere,
move in the passageways
of the self.
They are like shafts of light,
always changing, and you change
when you explore them.*

Rumi

say so, but I know he/she doesn't want me to do it."

None of these are true reasons not to change, but they sure put up a good line of resistance.

You might have noticed that nowhere on this list did you read, "I *don't know* what I want to change." Why? Because deep inside of us we always know what we want to change, but we use these other reasons to stop ourselves from moving ahead. It would be more likely, then, that "I know what I want, but I don't know how to do it or how to get started. And it's kind of scary just thinking about it."

At the moment of choice, we think we only have three options:
1. Yes
2. No
3. I don't know

This is not true; we have many creative options: stay open, ask questions, accept help.

TOUCHSTONE:
The only way out is through.

As an example, in the winter of 1984, I was finishing my Master's Degree at the University of Nebraska at Omaha, I went in to meet with my advisor to discuss the last classes I had to choose to complete my degree the next semester. My advisor, Mary, showed me the list of class options. I told her that there had to be a different way to graduate, because the options weren't very appealing. I had been working in the health care field for eight years to that point, in *many* different social service positions. I found that, although I was getting a graduate degree in social work in just five months, I was bored and frustrated with my experiences in the field.

Mary was open and flexible to my objections. She said, "Okay, let's look at this another way. Where do you see yourself in 10 years?" There was no question in my mind. I answered immediately, "I see myself living in the mountains, in a stone-wood home, with a male-partner person (I've never said "husband" or "marriage" well!), presenting seminars and workshops, writing books, being known internationally, making millions of dollars and not leaving home too often."

After a moment on "stun," Mary leaned back in her chair and burst into laughter. Then she looked at me and said, "You're serious, aren't you?" I said, "Yes. I know that I can do it. I just *don't know how* to get there from here." Mary composed herself and jumped right in to support my vision. She helped me set up a "Special Studies" class called: The Development and Implementation of Seminars and Workshops. I was supervised by Hobe, another professor, and started putting together the programs that I have been offering ever since.

TOUCHSTONE:
Just because you don't know how to "get there from here," doesn't mean you can't start asking questions and digging in to find out how you might get started.

Suffice to say, I live in Denver (closer to the mountains than Omaha), I am internationally known for my seminars and workshops, and this is my first book. (I'm working on the stone-wood home, male-partner person and the million dollars!) You've got to start somewhere!

TOUCHSTONE:
The world is out to "help" you.

EXERCISE:
Write out the answers to the following questions:

1. What or where is the "there" you would like to get to?
2. What don't you know that is stopping you?
3. Who can you ask to find out how to get there from here?
4. Who might have the answers?

PAYOFFS AND PRICE TAGS

A lot of what moves us to change is the weight of the payoff—what I will get out of the change—or the price tag—what it will cost me to change. Is the payoff—the "goodies"—for staying the way you are greater than the price tag? Then it's easy to stay put. Payoffs might include: feeling safe, feeling secure, maintaining the status quo, not having to risk and possibly fail and others. But if the price tag—pain, discomfort, etc.—becomes greater than the payoff, we tend to move toward reevaluating our situation, a move toward change.

*You will do foolish things,
but do them with enthusiasm.*

Colette
French writer (1873-1954)

Do something—even if it's wrong.

My Dad

EXERCISE:
Write a list of all the changes you are aware of that you need, want, wish, should do, have to do, or ought to do. Now, look over your list. What is keeping you from doing them? What are your reasons or excuses not to change? What are you waiting for?

TOUCHSTONE:
Life's too short not to live it.

To change and risk to move out of our comfort zone is very seldom easy, but not doing it, and living a life of regret, is much more painful in the long run.

Change, a bit at a time, is easier for some. Others store it all up and leap out into life with an enthusiasm that surprises even them. Whatever works for you is fine. I believe (my mental model) that part of the goal in life itself is to be open to and create healthy, positive change. In so doing, creating the life you want is truly a gift to yourself.

Movement is the natural state of nature. Take steps to keep your life in a balanced movement toward your true Self.

The key to release, rest, and inner freedom is not the elimination of all external difficulties. It is the letting go of our pattern of reactions to those difficulties.

Hugh Prather
*The Little Book
of Letting Go*

EXERCISE:
Write a list of everything you already know you can do to create change and a positive difference in your life. From this list, choose one item that you can accomplish in the next seven days and commit to following through on it. Then choose another, and so on.

PERSONAL RESPONSIBILITY

If you ever find yourself saying, "I don't know" about something, stop and ask yourself, "If I did know, what would it be?" It's a great "mind-jogger" to stimulate forward, proactive motion. This question reminds us we can choose to be responsible and accountable. For people who do not want to be accountable and responsible, believing and saying "I don't know" maintains the status quo in what may feel like a safe, though limiting, condition.

Stating "I don't know" can also be a barrier to keep others away. I worked as a live-in counselor in an adolescent girls group home in one of my "past life" jobs. Jill, one of the girls, had a major attitude problem. Her answer to almost everything was "whatever" and "I don't know." By shrugging off responsibility, she kept others away and kept herself in trouble with about everyone. Since I had only been in my job a day or two, I didn't have rapport with the girls. They knew they could play a lot of games with me until I understood the system. Jill decided that no matter what question I asked her, her answer, with one of those "wonderful" attitudes attached to it, would be, "I don't know." Later, when it came time for her to ask permission from me to use the phone, I answered, "I don't know," combined with a well performed shrug. All of the girls stood with their jaws wide open. They hadn't had this response from one of the professional "adults" before. Every time Jill asked me for or about anything that night, my answer and attitude was consistent: "I don't know." Finally, she "got it." She apologized and said that she didn't like being treated this way. Her mental models ran deep, so her behavior change didn't last long, but Jill realized that two could play the game of irresponsibility.

TAKE CHARGE

In order to deal effectively with transitions in life, it's important to take control of your thoughts about change and taking risks. Transitions will ask you to change, a little or a lot. Sometimes the transitions are inner change: the feelings, loyalties and beliefs we have about ourselves and our world. Other times transitions are outer change: a physical move, a body transformation, a relationship change, actions and behaviors that others can see and many more. You always have a choice. The fact remains, however, that no matter whether the change looks like it is an inner change or an outer change, it is always inner.

There are many different ways to perceive change. When change is seen as uninvited and threatening, it is "crisis." Since much of our reaction to life and life transitions is due to the words we use, consider this: There is no one word or character for our word *crisis* in the Chinese language. They use a combination of characters to make up crisis—the word *danger* and the word *opportunity*. To the Chinese, change is a "dangerous opportunity."

TOUCHSTONE:
Life is easier if you learn to embrace change more readily.

*Rabbi Zusya of Hanipol
used to say,
"If they ask me in the next world,
'Why were you not Moses?'
I will know the answer.
But if they ask me,
'Why were you not Zusya?'
I will have nothing to say."*

Martin Buber

*You gotta wonder why,
after disaster strikes,
we always say, "Boy, am I lucky."
It should be the normal day,
when you wake up,
go to work, come back and
nothing happens—
those are the days
you should say,
"Boy, am I lucky."*

Dave Barry
Humorist

Letting go, detaching and growing is not a linear, thinking process, it is an emotional one. The following are guides to what each of us goes through in the process of change and transition, as well as loss and the process of grief.

THE 7 STAGES OF CHANGE AND TRANSITION[9]

1. **DESTABILIZING AND LOSING FOCUS**
    When an event happens we tend to block it out mentally for seconds and sometimes even years. We can go through shock, numbness, feelings of unreality, loss of focus, "loss" in general, feeling off balance, feeling overwhelmed or immobilized. We can have difficulty making plans, concentrating, keeping in perspective.

    TOUCHSTONE:
    Stability in life is an illusion; we are constantly experiencing change and transitions.

2. **MINIMIZING THE IMPACT**
    In order to deal with pain and loss, we can go into denial. We attempt to return to "business as usual" to minimize the impact of the change.

    TOUCHSTONE:
    Learn to tell yourself the truth and build courage through judicious risk-taking.

3. **QUESTIONING SELF-WORTH**
    Over time, denial and minimization become less functional and reality of the transition sinks in. There can be a growing sense of depression, fear, powerlessness, occasional bursts of anger, out-of-control feelings, disillusionment, self-doubt and self-questioning.

TOUCHSTONE:
When in transition it's okay to feel down and angry, let yourself "feel." The harder one tries to get over it, the longer it seems to last.

4. **LETTING GO OF THE PAST**
    At some point, you must tell yourself the "truth" about the new reality and consciously choose to assume responsibility for the future. It is important to deal effectively with guilt and remorse issues that may arise. See yourself in the future, create short- and long-term action steps and goals to move on and out of the past and what was.

TOUCHSTONE:
The greatest power we have is to be self-determining.

5. **TESTING THE NEW SITUATION**
    This is an exciting stage. We can test ourselves in the unfolding new reality. Self-validation comes from trying out new behaviors and enveloping new skills.

TOUCHSTONE:
Growing self-confidence arises from acknowledging that we determine our own paths in life.

6. **SEARCHING FOR MEANING**
    While moving on, it is important to take time to reflect, to figure out the implications of the transition for one's life as a whole.

    Reflection offers us the following:

    ❧ A deeper insight into the way we deal with change; how it affects our relationship with ourselves, our work and other people.

    ❧ A time to strengthen our self-esteem and to stand back from the situation and view it from a more objective perspective.

❧ The development of a greater awareness of one's true and higher purpose in life.

7. **INTEGRATING THE EXPERIENCE**
Incorporate your discoveries and experience into everyday life. Relating to the world in new, more confident ways so that over time it becomes almost second hand, not stopping to think about it, *is* our natural state of being.

A whole person is one who has both walked with God and wrestled with the devil.

C. G. Jung

Chapter 5

TRANSITION

Not in his goals but in his transitions man is great.

Ralph Waldo Emerson

Life is an ongoing process of transition, of overlapping endings and beginnings. The more we understand this and embrace the process, change and transition become less threatening and less overwhelming.

William Bridges, in his book *Managing Transitions,* identifies the following three-stage process regarding the overlapping movement of change and transition:
1. The ending.
2. The neutral zone (a period of confusion and distress).
3. The new beginning.[10]

THE ENDING
The starting point of transition is the ending that you will have to make to leave the old situation behind. I often call this process of ending something making a "completion." When we complete something we close the file, the door, the energy or the life of the person, place or thing. Situational change hinges on letting go of the old things or relationships to let in the new. But psychological transitions depend on letting go of the old reality, mental model, and the old identity you had before the change took place.

*All changes,
even the most longed for,
have their melancholy;
for what we leave behind
is part of ourselves;
we must die to one life
before we can enter
into another.*

Anatole France Thibault
French writer

THE NEUTRAL ZONE: THE VOID

Once you've left the old mental model behind, you move on to the second step that comes after the letting go: the neutral zone. This is the no-man's-land between the old reality and the new. It is the limbo time when the old way is gone and the new doesn't feel comfortable yet. Have you ever felt like this? It can certainly be frustrating and stressful. A kind of emotional wilderness, a time when it isn't clear who you are or what is real. Painful though it often is, the neutral zone is the best stage for creativity, renewal and development. It is this gap between the old and the new that opens up the possibility of innovation and the beginning of revitalization.[11]

THE BEGINNING

Then comes the third step in transition: the beginning. People make the new beginning only if they have first made an ending, completed where they have been and spent some time in the neutral zone.

TOUCHSTONE:
Beginnings depend on endings.

Some transitional situations happen "to" us, others are of our choosing. When you choose your transition, it's much easier to minimize the importance of the endings and any frustrations and confusion through the transition period. If it was an exciting venture, like getting married (ending single life) or quitting an uninteresting job for a better one, the ending was something looked forward to, possibly even a relief. If the ending was painful but still consciously chosen, some may feel that to acknowledge that the ending hurt would be to admit that the transition was wrong or a mistake.[12]

IDENTITY

The paradox of letting go and moving on to new beginnings is grounded in our issues of identity. It is amazing how we will hold on to outdated beliefs and identities, prolonging our transition into the new even when it's painful to do so. The following story relates this "holding on" issue well.

The old radio comedian, Bob Burns ("The Arkansas Traveler"), used to tell the story of eating Army food for the first time after 18 years of his mother's deep-fat frying. A week of the bland GI fare was enough to cure something that he had never known he had: a lifelong case of heartburn. Rather than feeling relief at this improvement, Burns said he rushed into the dispensary, clutching his stomach and yelling, "Doc, Doc! Help me! I'm dying. My fire went out!"[13]

We come to identify ourselves with the circumstances of our lives. Our identity—who we think we are—is partly defined by the roles and relationships that we have. Over a lifetime we have consciously and unconsciously developed within and adjusted to fit a given life pattern. The road to changing "who we are" is much rougher than we think.

Have you ever heard this said, "Watch out for what you pray for, you might get it and you may not want it." Lottery winners are a good example of the amazing strength of conditioned beliefs and identity and the incredible power of the conditioned unconscious. In *USA Today* several years ago, there was a story about a 37-year-old fry cook with a wife and two children who had won a $3.6 million lottery. Within two weeks of his exciting life-changing experience, he died of a heart attack. His widow told the paper that he was physically fine *before* he won the money. She said that the stress and confusion of that much money was so overwhelming he died.

What's wrong with this picture? He didn't *prepare* himself for the change. He hadn't gotten "ready" for the money. He bought lottery tickets with hopes of winning and probably with doubt that he would. But he didn't take the time to "change his identity," mentally or otherwise, to get psychologically ready for the change to the new financial status. Basically, the instant wealth overloaded his circuits. It was too far out of his normal realm of thinking and believing about himself, his identity.

Please, God, give me the chance to prove that winning the lottery won't spoil me!

Refrigerator magnet

EXERCISE:
Get ready for your new identity—your "new normal". In your mind's eye picture:

1. *How* would you like your life to be different?
2. *Who* would you like to be in your new identity and future?
3. *What* would be different from what you have and who you are today?
4. *What* relationships in your life would change?
5. *What* changes in your job, your life-style, the way you dress, the food you eat, your home, your car, etc., would you make?

Now write down these "new normals." How does it feel? Does it fit or is it uncomfortable?

In our culture, money is part of our mental model and identity regarding issues of security, freedom, importance and the "I've made

*Nothing we ever imagined is
beyond our powers,
only beyond our present
self-knowledge.*

Theodore Roszak

it" beliefs and attitudes. Using the lottery example, what have you said about such a possible experience? "Oh yeah, just let me win that money, I'd have a great time." You might consider whether you have done your part to get ready for the changes it would bring into your life. I have heard lottery winners, people who have inherited substantial amounts of money and others who have come into finances that changed their lives describe this experience as a burden. They have commented, "It takes a lot of time and energy to manage this money!" It became quite a different *picture* than what they had bargained for.

Here is a perfect example, from the daily paper as I am writing this book. Newspaper headline "Lotto winner torches home." A 32-year-old man in Ohio had set fire to the $170,000 house he'd built with part of the 1986 $7.5 million lottery winnings he collected. Why? He testified in court that winning the jackpot had made his life "a living hell" because people were demanding money from him. Before winning the lottery, he earned $14,000 a year at a home improvement center. He snapped. He is on two years' probation.

The next time you think or hear "Watch out for what you pray for, you might get it and you may not want it," remember, you can say "no thank you" and let it go. Or, you can plan ahead.

PLAN AHEAD

It is said that we don't plan to fail, we fail to plan. Your job is not to push away growth, change and prosperity in any area of life, but to plan ahead. Do you want more money in your life? Take a few financial management courses to make sure you understand how to manage it when it gets here. Do you want a healthy love relationship? Take some classes, be around healthy couples, do things that will set you up to be the healthiest *you* can be to meet your objective. Take the time to clean out your conditioned mental closets to get psychologically ready for any changes you would like to "see" come into your life. That *is* your job.

I presented a seminar on developing healthy relationships where the audience tended to be openly cynical and sarcastic about there being any healthy men or women in the world to date or marry. Like this book, the class was about self-management skills—doing your job to get your world in order first. At the end of the program I handed out a contract form to each participant. It stated, "I name deserve the best, healthiest relationship possible. I name will create this relationship by date ." No one signed the form. When I asked why, the participants explained that they now understood that they had a lot of personal work to do on themselves first. Then they asked me if I was going to sign the form. I said "No. But then I'm not complaining."

TOUCHSTONE:
If you don't know who you are and what you want, who does?

Taking time to think, write and talk about what you want is important. It's important to dream and wonder and wander and imagine the greatest life you can for yourself. Again, if you don't do it, who will? If not now...when? Don't wait another day. Start planning, and replanning. Take action on your plans no matter what the level of your self-confidence. Action begets action. And courage begets courage. Your future is your next breath.

Then, when all the great stuff you planned for starts to happen, DON'T SCARE YOURSELF! Enjoy it! What if someone says, about your good experiences, "Must be nice!" Your answer is, "It is!" You're not taking anything away from anyone living a full life. There's plenty to go around.

EXERCISE:
Write a list of ways that you can "get ready" for new identities for your life. Identity areas might include:

Finance changes.

Job title / position.

Retirement.

Moving.

Different or healthier relationships.

Divorce.

Widowhood.

Healthier physical body.

Weight loss.

If you know what you want, you will recognize it when you see it.

Bill Cosby

Pregnancy.

Different life-style.

Graduation from school / college / military.

Return from military duty.

Healthy, happier attitude.

Add your own . . .

TOUCHSTONE:
We don't plan to fail, we fail to plan.

*A step in the wrong direction
is better than staying
on the spot all your life.
Once you're moving forward
you can correct your course
as you go.
Your automatic guidance system
cannot guide you when you're
standing still.*

Maxwell Maltz

Chapter 6

THE SHADOW

*The shadow of one culture
is a tinderbox of trouble for another.*

Robert A. Johnson
Owning Your Own Shadow

"Do as I say, not as I do" is an age-old command to children. We all, as children, learned by example and by the roles others played in our lives. We developed our mental models by mimicking, honoring and obeying, and playing games just like *those people* we admired, loved or feared. While visiting a friend recently, some neighbor girls came over to play. The game of mimic for the afternoon was "wedding." They got out dolls and cars and everything they could find to create an adult world mirror. One of the girls, Gail, about nine years old, dressed a doll as the bride to be and sat her in the back of the car. She pushed the car around talking out loud for the doll looking for her groom. "Well, where is he again? Late for our wedding. He's probably out drinking again. Well, I'll have to change him later." And on she went, pushing her lone bride around in her car.

Whose script is this? The doll's? Of course not, it is Gail's script. It is what her world has offered her for mental model conditioning. It's not right or wrong, it just is. That's all she knows. It is the truth for her.

Gail lives in a home with parents and extended family members who are alcoholics. Gail sometimes would talk about how scary it was to

We don't know who we are, and that who we think of as ourselves is an illusion given to us and maintained by society.

John Provost
on Thomas Merton's
"false self"

ride in the car with her parents when they were drinking. Her younger sister, about four years old, added, "Never drink and drive. Never."

MENTAL PROGRAMMING AND CONDITIONING

TOUCHSTONE:
70 percent of all mental programming is achieved by age six and perhaps as much as 95 percent of the continued mental conditioning is completed by age 14.

Many behavior experts agree that by the age of 10 children are mentally conditioned to be who they're going to be in life. To change any of this programming takes much more work than having absorbed better information the first time around.

TOUCHSTONE:
We believe what we are programmed to believe.

During the first 18 years of our lives, if we grew up in fairly average, reasonably positive homes, we were told "No!" or what we could *not* do more than *148,000 times!* If you were a little more fortunate, you may have been told "No!" only 100,000 times or 50,000 times—however many, it was considerably more negative programming than any of us needs.[14]

What about positive strokes and programming during those first 18 years? There are scores of people who cannot remember being told what they *could* accomplish in life more than three or four times![15] Whatever the number, for most of us the "yes's" we received simply didn't balance out the "no's." The occasional words of belief and true encouragement were just that—occasional—and they were far outweighed by our daily doses of "cannot's."

Even though as much as 75 percent of everything we think is negative, counterproductive and works against us, we also know that much of this negative programming was well intentioned. Think about your parents, grandparents or whoever did the major part of raising you as a child. What was their programming? Where did they learn about self-esteem and positive mental programming issues? A few seconds on these two questions alone will help you pull back from blame and criticism of what they did or didn't do with, to and for you, and draw out compassion instead. They did the best they could with what they had at the time.

SHADOW

Our early programming builds the foundation for what is called the "shadow," that part of us we fail to see or know. It is a Jungian Psychotherapy term for the hundreds of internalized interpretations of others' beliefs, thoughts, rules, judgments and fears.

Our *ego* is the part of us that we are and know about consciously. Our *persona* is the mask we present as our image to the world, that which we would like to be and how we wish to be seen. The *shadow* is the dark side. It is the heap of refused, unacknowledged and unacceptable characteristics we push down and try to ignore in order to maintain a consistent identity. Because we want to be accepted, this consistent identity keeps us from being rejected from our peers, family and society. When hidden long enough, these dark side characteristics take on a life of their own—the shadow life.[16]

There are many people who seem to "have it all together." They may have happy faces, the right jobs, 2.5 children. They may be funny and seem to enjoy life, the *persona* that says they fit in, are acceptable and are safe. But because inside they feel like they don't fit in, they live with feelings of inadequacy and fear, the *not good enough's*, in paranoia and guilt. They fear that "Someone is going to find out *who I really am* and they won't like me. They'll find out that I'm an imposter."

Sometimes people with this pent up, suppressed guilt and fear come off angry, rageful, abusive, cynical, prejudicial, critical or self-righteous. Having compassion and clear boundaries with these kinds of people is not always an easy task. It's easier to mirror back to them their limited scope of life in just as unbalanced a manner. How did they get this way?

CONDITIONING

We come into the world as blank slates. Over time, through our daily lives with family mentors, role models and close relationships, as well as unconscious programming from television, radio, advertising and others' perceptions and judgments of life, like pliable clay we get molded. We take on others' pain and shame and unfinished life business. One more generation gets it. Don't reach for the prozac just yet! There's hope.

*We all are born whole
but somehow the culture
demands that we live out only
part of our nature
and refuse other parts
of our inheritance.
We divide the self into an ego
and a shadow
because our culture insists that
we behave in
a particular manner.*

Robert A. Johnson
Owning Your Own Shadow

Life is full of overflowing with the new. But it is necessary to empty out the old to make room for the new to enter.

Eileen Caddy
Footprints on the Path

SHADOW BOXING

The following illustrations (Figures 2-7) came to me last year as I was going through a dark time, trying to figure out what my beliefs on several issues were and where I learned them. When drawn out, this picture helped me visualize my *cleaning out* of some shadow issues unconsciously given to me by others throughout my life.

Each figure represents where we are in our evolution with the shadow.

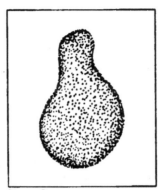

Figure 2

STEP #1—BELIEFS:

In childhood, we become a product of our environment. We learn about the world through others' beliefs, perceptions and conditioned programming. We take on others' shadows, unaware that it is happening. It is the ongoing input and information we receive from all around us each day.

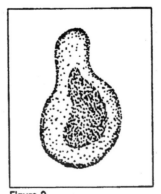

Figure 3

STEP #2—IDENTITY:

We become a product of our environment. We "identify" with the people, things, routines, language, dress and such of those around us— that which is normal. We can repeat the language and thoughts, duplicate gestures, and automatically follow routines and ritual. We are all the same—"this" way—our mental model.

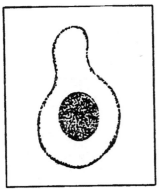

Figure 4

STEP #3—EVENTS:
We notice that others have different beliefs and behaviors from ours and our families. We are somewhat conscious that we are repeating these conditioned beliefs. Others may even ask that we stop being or doing something that we have been taught was right and okay or to start being or doing what they have learned. We may think and ask, "Oh, you mean it's *not* this way? There are *other* ways?" The polarity, we/they, begins. *We* are *this* way, *they* are *that* way. *We* are *right*, *they* are *wrong*.

Figures 2-4 (Steps 1-3) are unconscious conditioning throughout childhood.

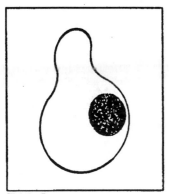

Figure 5

STEP #4—QUESTION:
Our *individuation process*, the creating of our own identity, begins when we start to ask questions. We want to understand and see for ourselves, breaking away from "the way it always is," the unquestioned. "Why...." and "What if...." are important questions

asked at this time. "What if *we aren't right?*" "What if *they aren't wrong?*"

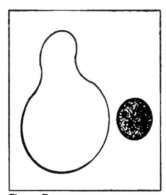

Figure 6

*It is more disrupting to find out
that you have a
profound nobility of character
than to find out you are a bum.*

Robert A. Johnson
Owning Your Own Shadow

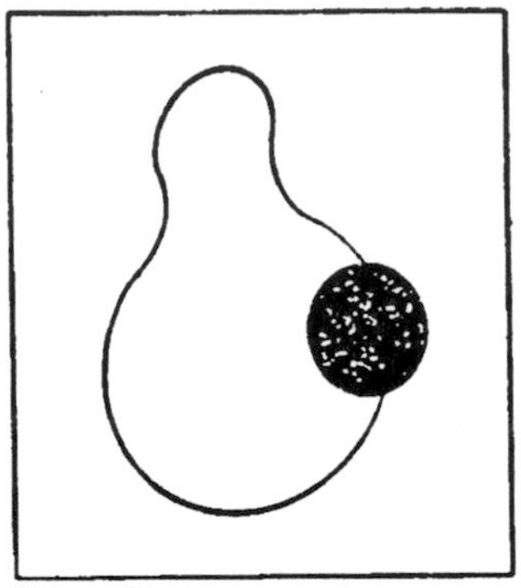

STEP #5—TRANSITION:
We start to feel some change and freedom from the old belief and to realize what the new belief can be. "Let's look at alternatives and options, other ways of doing, of being." This is the transition of identity, individuation. New beliefs alter one's view of self and the world.

Figure 7

*If we could read the secret history
of our enemies,
we should find in each man's life
sorrow and suffering enough to
disarm all hostility.*

Henry Wadsworth Longfellow

STEP #6—SHIFT/REDECIDE:
"Oh!"—The *shift*, moving the old belief "out of yourself." It is not yours, it never was. You clean it off and out of yourself to find the *Self* you are meant to be.

Figures 5-7 (Steps 4-6) are conscious steps from the "false, ego self" to your "true, core Self."

Though you may work out one shadow issue, there are others lurking behind to be brought up in conscious awareness and shifted out. Struggle, attachment, and the *dark night* experience in this illustration is between steps 5 and 6. You can see what the difference can be if you redecide to change; but, due to past conditioned fear and

BORDERS

BORDERS
BOOKS MUSIC AND CAFE
#441

STORE: 0441   REG: 05/73   TRAN#: 1913
SALE   05/31/2004   EMP: 01264

LETTING GO WITH ALL YOUR MIGHT
        7185781   OP T   18.95
SPANISH NOW LEVEL 1-E06
        4825142   OP T   16.95

              Subtotal   35.90
              COLORADO 7.2%   2.58
2 Items   Total   38.48
              VISA   38.48
ACCT # /S XXXXXXXXXXXX0823
              AUTH: 083959
NAME: BRAYMAN/KIMBERLY

           CUSTOMER COPY

        05/31/2004 05:29PM

        Thank you for shopping at
           Borders in Longmont!
              www.borders.com

the item during the 12 month period prior to the return will be refunde
via a gift card.

Opened videos, discs, and cassettes may only be exchanged fo
replacement copies of the original item.
Periodicals, newspapers, out-of-print, collectible and pre-owned item
may not be returned.
Returned merchandise must be in saleable condition.

BORDERS

Merchandise presented for return, including sale or marked-down items,
must be accompanied by the original Borders store receipt. Returns must
be completed within 30 days of purchase. The purchase price will be
refunded in the medium of purchase (cash, credit card or gift card). Items
purchased by check may be returned for cash after 10 business days.

Merchandise unaccompanied by the original Borders store receipt, or
presented for return beyond 30 days from date of purchase, must be
carried by Borders at the time of the return. The lowest price offered for
the item during the 12 month period prior to the return will be refunded
via a gift card.

Opened videos, discs, and cassettes may only be exchanged for
replacement copies of the original item.
Periodicals, newspapers, out-of-print, collectible and pre-owned items
may not be returned.
Returned merchandise must be in saleable condition.

BORDERS®

Merchandise presented for return, including sale or marked-down items,
must be accompanied by the original Borders store receipt. Returns must
be completed within 30 days of purchase. The purchase price will be
refunded in the medium of purchase (cash, credit card or gift card). Items
purchased by check may be returned for cash after 10 business days.

Merchandise unaccompanied by the original Borders store receipt, or
presented for return beyond 30 days from date of purchase, must be
carried by Borders at the time of the return. The lowest price offered for
the item during the 12 month period prior to the return will be refunded
via a gift card.

Opened videos, discs, and cassettes may only be exchanged for
replacement copies of the original item.
Periodicals, newspapers, out-of-print, collectible and pre-owned items
may not be returned.
Returned merchandise must be in saleable condition.

BORDERS

****

ET A $20 GIFT CARD

Get the card that rewards you with
ints toward books, music, and movies
every time you use it.

Call 1-800-294-0038 to apply for the
Borders and Waldenbooks Visa Card
today and get a $20 Gift Card after
your first purchase with the card!

For complete details, please visit
www.borders.bankone.com

X

STORE: REG: 05/73   TRAN#: 1913
SALE: 05/31/2004   EMP: 01264
****

BORDERS

Merchandise presented for return, including sale or marked-down item must be accompanied by the original Borders store receipt. Returns m be completed within 30 days of purchase. The purchase price will refunded in the medium of purchase (cash, credit card or gift card). Ite purchased by check may be returned for cash after 10 business days.

Merchandise unaccompanied by the original Borders store receipt, presented for return beyond 30 days from date of purchase, must carried by Borders at the time of the return. The lowest price offered the item during the 12 month period prior to the return will be refund via a gift card.

Opened videos, discs, and cassettes may only be exchanged replacement copies of the original item.
Periodicals, newspapers, out-of-print, collectible and pre-owned item may not be returned.
Returned merchandise must be in saleable condition.

BORDERS

Merchandise presented for return, including sale or marked-down items, must be accompanied by the original Borders store receipt. Returns mus be completed within 30 days of purchase. The purchase price will be refunded in the medium of purchase (cash, credit card or gift card). Items purchased by check may be returned for cash after 10 business days.

beliefs, it is easy to get stuck here.

Is the shadow always negative? No. Astonishingly enough, some very good characteristics also turn up in the shadow. Ordinary, mundane characteristics tend to be the norm and anything less than this goes into the shadow. But anything better also goes into the shadow!

GOLD

Some of the *pure gold* of our personalities are relegated to the shadow because it can find no place to "shine" in our experiences with family, society and culture. Interestingly enough, to draw out and deal with the skeletons in our closets is relatively easy, but to "own the gold" in the shadow is terrifying. It is easier and safer to stay where we feel comfortable than to be free, to feel better or to have a more positive life.

The 6-step illustration of moving old unconscious programming out can also be used to move the "gold," the new, conscious programming in. Invert the six steps so that you start with number 6 and go to number 1. Decide what new belief you want to integrate and move it into your thoughts, words, conversations, routine, ritual and relationships. Start seeing yourself this new way. Over time, you will "become" this new belief or identity (Figure 2). It will be your "new normal," the new you. It is actually more true to say that accepting the "gold" is *coming home* to the original unprogrammed you.

JUDGMENT

While I was waiting in a fast-food restaurant one day, a woman in her early 20's walked in. She had on army boots, a skirt, several layered tops and a jean jacket. Her hair was long on one side and shaved to the skull on the other. A tattoo graced her head and a bunch of pierced earrings dangled from one ear. My immediate reaction was to judge her, put her into my box of labels and at-arms-length descriptions *to make us different*. I caught myself doing it, became aware of my mental model chatter and stopped. I redecided to not dump my shadow on her and project my fears or issues. I thought, "I don't know who she is, she may be one of the nicest, gentlest, most intelligent, talented people around. Let it go." My body relaxed, and I ordered my food.

*The mind is its own place,
and in itself,
can make a heaven of hell
or a hell of heaven.*

John Milton
(1608-1674)

TOUCHSTONE:
It is not what happens to us or around us that matters; it is how we act or react that rules our lives.

EXERCISE:
Take a few minutes to write answers to the following questions:

1. What "shadow" characteristics do you have?
2. Which of these are you ready to move out?
3. What is your buried gold?
4. What new identity characteristics would you like to develop?

FEAR OF SELF

Sabotaging ourselves is one way to bury our gold. What would stop you from shining, upgrading your identity? Have you heard of *fear of success*? Fear of success is much more common and threatening than fear of failure. We fail and make mistakes every day. The gold in the shadow is related to our life's purpose, our *higher calling*. If you have felt unworthy, frustrated and critical of yourself for years, your higher calling can be hard to accept. Ignoring the gold can be as damaging as ignoring the dark side. Some people may suffer a severe shock or illness, a "wake-up call," before they learn how to let the gold out.[16]

TIME AND EXPERIENCE

Examples of great leaders and teachers of the world who took years to clean out the shadow in order to let their gold shine are numerous. Many of the world's well-known and revered scholars and mystics leaped full steam into life only after they were 40 years of age or older. They heard the "calling" for years—to be, to do, and to have what they were here for—but through their own fears and conditioned shadow beliefs, they found many reasons to push their *light* away through procrastination, illness and other creative conscious and unconscious maneuvers.

Whether it's the 20th or the 12th century, America or Budapest, self-doubt and fear are the same. Hildegard of Bingen (Germany, 1098-1179) was an abbess, poetess, prophet, reformer, artist, musician, healer, scientist and mystical theologian. She was also a child born into a culture, a mental model, that did not support women.

*What you think of me
is none of my business.*

Terry Cole-Whittaker

Book Title

Hildegard was a woman in a patriarchal culture and a male-run church who strove to be heard, who struggled to offer her own wisdom and gifts borne of experience and suffering of women of the past. In a letter to St. Bernard of Clairvaux, she complained of the burden she carried as a woman in a patriarchal culture. She struggled for years with "I can't" or "I shouldn't" or "Who am I to..." thoughts and feelings that she had been taught.[17]

Hildegard, though prolific throughout her life, was often confined to a sickbed because she succumbed to this covering up of her talents and her voice (her gold). Her conversion out of the shadow, at age 42, was to redecide, to trust her "Self" and the process, and to take the leap into writing and speaking her visions for the larger community. She took command of her vocation and creative life for 40 more years.

Do you ever worry about what others will think of you? You're in good company. Patrick of Ireland (actually *not* Irish, but from England) is another great teacher, leader and mystic in our world who stayed stuck in limiting thoughts and fears of inadequacy for the better part of his life.

Patrick's story is that of a man who was called and tried to say no. Patrick resisted the call of the Spirit for 18 years. He procrastinated, he wandered around Europe, he protested his inadequacy; in fact, he did everything possible to avoid God's wish that he preach to the Irish. In his book *Confession*, St. Patrick says, "...I long had in mind to write, but hesitated until now; I was afraid of exposing myself to the talk of men, because I have not studied like the others.... I blush and fear exceedingly to reveal my lack of education."[18]

Patrick returned to Ireland at age 40, ancient by the standards of his time, to begin the mission he never wanted to do. He returned only after spending 18 years fighting his inner "calling" and doing what he saw as preparing, through studies of many kinds, to feel adequate.

Gandhi, at 50, discovered his life mission. Julia Child began her successful TV career after 50. Winston Churchill became prime minister at 65, and Margaret Thatcher prime minister at 53. Like these examples of powerfully conscious individuals, many others have spent their lives moving through and moving out the shadow, conditioned beliefs and perceptions of the outside world, incubating and percolating their way home to themselves later in life.

PERSONAL RESPONSIBILITY

Healing, letting go of conditioned beliefs, is each person's responsibility. There is no one *out there* past, present or future who can do it for us. I know many people who have read all the self-help books, listened to self-improvement tapes, have been analyzed, therapized and scrutinized by some of the best. They are only missing one key ingredient to the mixture of developmental change— their own mental model shift and redecisions to change. This kind of lifelong search for one's "treasure in one's own backyard" has been labeled by some as "educated ignorance." You know what's wrong and can even tell others exactly what it is, but you won't take the steps to do what is needed—you won't take the leap.

Beneath the fear of our death is the fear of looking into ourselves, because death is like a mirror in which the true meaning of life is reflected. In the face of death you realize what is the most important thing in life.

Sogyal Rinpoche
Author of *The Tibetan Book of Living and Dying*

FACING FEAR

There was a great white elephant in Africa, so the story goes. The people of the village wanted this magnificent elephant. They planned to train him to be one of their working animals, to clear brush and move rock. They organized many hunts to capture this animal, finally succeeding. The elephant was tied up in leg irons, chained and whipped into submission to do their work. After several months of this painful experience, the elephant broke his chains and ran away from the village. The hunters chased him for many days.

When the elephant was thirsty or hungry, tired or weary from running, he would stop and rest. At the slightest rustle of brush, however, he would bolt from his rest and run until he was exhausted. This went on for years for fear that the hunters would catch him again and take him back to be chained and beaten.

One day, a wood nymph climbed down from a tree near where the elephant was resting and whispered in his ear, "Why are you running? There is no one chasing you anymore, they quit long ago. You are now only running from your own fear."

The real problem is not the individual's ability to have a good life, it's his capacity not to have one.

Thomas Moore
Care of the Soul

EXERCISE:
Draw a vertical line down the middle of a piece of paper. On the left hand side, write a list of answers to these questions.
1. What is it that you think about, dream about, wish that you could be, do or have?
2. What calling, inner pulling or gnawing do you have that you are not following?

On the right hand side, write:
1. Your fears, thoughts and beliefs that stop you from moving forward and acting on these ideas.*
2. What actions and behavior you take, what you are doing that stops you from moving ahead.

*Age, sex, race, finances, physical ability and looks don't count!

Acknowledge your blocks to forward movement and proactively choose to do something about them, or let them go.

There once was a man who always thought about being a lawyer, but he worked all his life in other jobs. When he retired at 68, he shared this dream with a friend. He admitted that he still thought about it, but felt he was now too old. At 68, he argued, it could take another 10 years to go to law school and who knew if he'd even pass the bar exam. In 10 years, by the time he finished, he'd be 78. His friend asked, "How old will you be in 10 years if you don't do it?"

TOUCHSTONE:
Age is not a good reason to not follow or to let go of your dreams. Nor are most of the excuses we give ourselves.

A movie video that I can't recommend highly enough is *A Brief History of Time*, the life story of physicist Stephan Hawking. A quick overview will not spoil the show: Stephan was born normal, healthy and extremely intelligent. He loved many topics in the fields of research, physics and such. He was "asked to leave" higher education on occasion due to his attitude. In his early 20's Hawking was diagnosed with Lou Gehrig's disease. Confined to a wheelchair for life, unable to speak or move, he learned to communicate through the use of a computer created specifically for him. He went on to teach as a professor in physics and to become the key researcher of the Black Hole of the universe. He is married, has three daughters and lives a full, wonderful life.

One of the highlights, among many in the documentary, is an interview with Hawkings' mother. She said that for Stephan to get a disease like this was actually a *good* thing. Although, she would never wish something like this on him or anyone else, it helped Stephan by limiting his ability to use his wondering thoughts and huge ideas. Since it required much of his energy just to stay alive, the disease made him stop and focus on only one thing that he could study, not on a thousand things that could not have received his attention at all.

FIVE DEVELOPMENTAL FACTORS THAT CONTROL OUR SUCCESS OR FAILURE.[19]

1. **Behavior**
   Our actions, what we do or don't do.
   Behavior or actions create results.

2. **Feelings**
   Every action we take is first filtered through our feelings. How we *feel* about something will always determine or affect what we *do* and how well we do it.

It's not what happens to you, it's what you do about it.

W Mitchell
Book, Video and Presentation

3. **Attitudes**
Our attitudes are the perspective from which we view our life.
Attitude = Feelings = Behavior

4. **Beliefs**
Beliefs = Attitude = Feelings = Actions

5. **Programming**
We believe what we are programmed to believe.

TOUCHSTONE:
Question everything.

EXERCISE:
Write down the following sentence starter and finish it as many times as you can (at least 50 times.)

❧ If I knew that I could not fail, I would . . . .

*One cannot conquer the evil
in himself by resisting it . . .
but by transmutting its energies
into other forms.
The energy that expresses itself in
the form of evil is the same
energy which expresses itself in
the form of good;
and thus the one may be
transmuted into the other.*

Charles Henry MacKintosh
I Looked On Life

III

The ReDecisions Model for Change and Transition

Rarely easy, work with the soul is usually
placed squarely in that place
we would rather not visit,
in that emotion we don't want to feel,
and in that understanding we would prefer to do without.
The most honest route may be the most difficult to take.
It is not easy to visit the place in ourselves
that is most challenging
and to look straight into the image that
gives us the most fright;
yet, there, where the work is most intense,
is the source of soul.

Thomas Moore
Care of the Soul

> *Metamorphosis doesn't happen*
> *without our artful participation.*
>
> Thomas Moore
> *Care of the Soul*

Chapter 7

THE REDECISIONS 11-STAGE MODEL

*Ain't it funny how we come in kickin' giddyup
and go out hollerin' whoa
We never want to be here
Sure don't ever want to go*

"Kickin' and Screamin'," lyrics by Tony Arata
Garth Brooks
In Pieces album

What nature in beauty and grace does season after season, year after year, through millenniums of time, we as human beings fight with tooth and nail. The transition of life, death and rebirth is a process as old as the universe itself. It is so unfortunate that most of us have lost what early man and native tribes, close to nature and the earth, understood so well, so naturally. They knew life/death/life cycle patterns are all around us, that the cycles are normal and natural, expected, useful and necessary for the greatest growth we can hope to experience.

TOUCHSTONE:
Without life there is no death; without death, no life.

As nature spends all of its energy in the natural ebb and flow of life cycles, one of our greatest life lessons is to learn to flow with change. We need to understand, expect, even welcome endings, feelings of emptiness and confusion, knowing that they will lead us to new beginnings, to rebirth, to our fresh new season.

THE REDECISIONS MODEL

The transformational overlap of beginnings, dark nights, endings and rebirth are constantly active in our world. Over the years, as I've worked with people to identify their part in their transitions and life/ work redecisions, I have identified specific stages and have created a model to help guide others through this process more easily.

I learn best through visual stimulus (seeing) and processing (talking out— even on my friends' answering machines!) my ideas, thoughts and feelings with others. Being a speaker and a writer is a good vocation for me. Since I know that I'm not the only one who learns best by "seeing" pictures to understand intellectual jargon, I have created the ReDecisions Model (Figure 8). This model helps explain how we deal with beliefs, transition, and mental models, how we stay stuck in them and how to learn to let go, move on and live in a more fluid way—to "shift" through mental changes and life transitions more easily.

This model has 11 clearly defined stages, including four expanded areas of understanding how the stages and our movement through them help develop our wholeness. I will add the title to each stage as it is defined, as well as to the slanted lines and to how the arrows and their differences relate.

Awakening begins when a man realizes that he is going nowhere and does not know where to go.

Georges Gurdjieff
Armenian author
and explorer
(1872-1949)

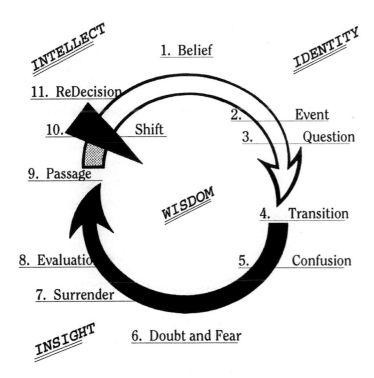

Figure 8 The ReDecisions 11-Stage Model

The redecision process (the life/death/life cycles, endings and beginnings) and letting go is not easy, though it is necessary. It is one over which we don't always have control.

This process of cleansing and transformation is similar to extracting gold from base matter. Through alchemical cooking the gold captured in base matter is brought out. Your gold is your own spiritual life that is clouded in the pure matter of your physical interests. Endings and beginnings in the process of transformation are to bring out or draw forth the gold of your spiritual character. There are no fast answers, "fixes" or magic pills to many of our transitions. You have to move into this slowly. This ordeal is a gradual clarification and purification of your life.[20]

A man must evelate himself by his own mind, not degrade himself. The mind is the friend of the conditioned soul, and his enemy as well.

Bhagavad——Gita VI:5

TOUCHSTONE:
Awakening to your "true Self" is your only job.

Think wrongly if you please,
but in all cases
think for yourself.

Louisa May Alcott

WAKE UP

A good example of this cleaning out process is played out on the silver screen is the 1990 Steven Spielberg movie, *Joe Versus the Volcano*. Joe Banks, played by Tom Hanks, reached a dead end in his job and in his life. He states, "I'm losing my soul," just before learning from his doctor that he has a terminal "brain cloud." The movie humorously depicts the almost constant "sleeping state" we live in, clouding up our gold, keeping us from waking up to our true Selves. When Joe meets Patricia (Meg Ryan), she shares her father's wisdom with him, shedding light on his terminal illness and providing answers to change and transformation. "My father says that almost the whole world is asleep—everybody you know, everybody you see, everybody you talk to. He says that only a few people are awake, and they live in a state of constant, total amazement."

EXERCISE:
Write out the answers to these questions for personal exploration.

1. What does your "true Self" look like?
2. What would it take to wake you up from your sleep?
3. What conditioned, limiting beliefs are clouding or keeping down the "gold" of your truest Self?
4. What would need to change in your life if you were to live from your true Self?

It doesn't matter what road you
take, hill you climb,
or path you're on,
you will always end up
in the same place,
learning.

Ralph Stevenson

Chapter 8

ENLIGHTENMENT AND ENDARKENMENT: THE ARROWS

*. . . life becomes death and death becomes life,
and darkness turns into light and light into
unbelievable darkness—
are there any limits to the amount of jesting
that goes on in the universe
or the number of surprises that stun us?*

Matthew Fox
Creation Spirituality

Life is a paradox, like a constantly flipping two-sided coin. We cannot have one side without the other. In a linear way, then, we divide life and its experiences into two parts: good or bad, right or wrong, black or white, all or none (Figure 9).

Figure 9

*One may not reach
the dawn save by
the path of the night.*

Kahlil Gibran
Sand and Foam

ENLIGHTENMENT

In the ReDecisions Model, the top arrow represents the *known: knowledge*. It is our present belief system, the mental model in which we are comfortable, safe and secure. It is the way life "should always be." It is the light, rainbow colors, sunny, bright and open. We feel conscious, enlightened, focused and right with the world when we feel in control and "connected."

ENDARKENMENT

The bottom arrow represents the *unknown:* confusion, doubt, fear, loss and grief. This is not where we like to spend our time. It feels dark, scary, unsafe and closed, like we are disconnected from the flow of life. If we could avoid it, in fact, that would be great.

TOUCHSTONE:
No one escapes the dark times.

Human beings have a great capacity to avoid pain, hurt, sadness and grief. We will go to almost any lengths to avoid "bad" feelings. However, to refuse to feel and experience these emotions can leave us with even more feelings that are uncomfortable, often leading to feelings of despair, hopelessness and meaninglessness. One can endure any suffering if it has meaning; but meaninglessness is unbearable. If we don't let ourselves "feel" *all* feelings, we are not living the full range of life. It is the paradox of life—the up and down, in and out, black and white— that makes us feel alive and offers creativity. It is a powerful embracing of reality.[21]

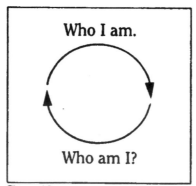

Figure 10

We might also see these arrows as discussed earlier, the eternal search for ourselves, our true identities. (Figure 10)

TOUCHSTONE:
The more light you realize, the more dark is at its opposite. This is true for all of life.

SELF-IMAGE

After 21 years in the same company, my friend Cathy felt discontent with her work and decided to go to a career counselor for guidance. Her homework assignment was to write down a list of her skills, talents and abilities that they could evaluate during her next session. Cathy is a brilliant, intelligent, educated, wonderful, beautiful person. This should have been an easy exercise. It was not. Cathy called me one night agonizing over what to write down. She said that what she did *anyone could do*, and she didn't see herself as skilled or talented in any special way. I asked her to take a piece of paper, write *my* name at the top, then write a list of skills and abilities she sees me as having. Cathy and I are a lot alike, so I knew she could come up with a good number of qualities. After she read me her list of how she saw me, I asked her to erase my name and put hers at the top instead. She was amazed.

Cathy's conditioned beliefs from family and her cultural background have taught her that she is second best, not deserving and doesn't count much. No matter what greatness she has to offer, it is hard for her to see it.

*God allows us to experience
the low points of life
in order to
teach us lessons we
could not learn in any other way.*

C. S. Lewis

EXERCISE:
On a piece of paper, create two columns. Title the left column, "Who I am." Write all those aspects of who you are: skills, abilities, personality and so on. These are the things that you know about yourself. Title the right side, "Who am I?" Find the "more" of who you really are and put it here. Think on a higher objective level about who your "true Self" is for the second column. If you get stuck, ask friends to help.

THE ICEBERG

Life is like an iceberg. There is a lot above water that we can see, but so much underneath that is seldom or never seen or realized, about ourselves and others. (Figure 11)

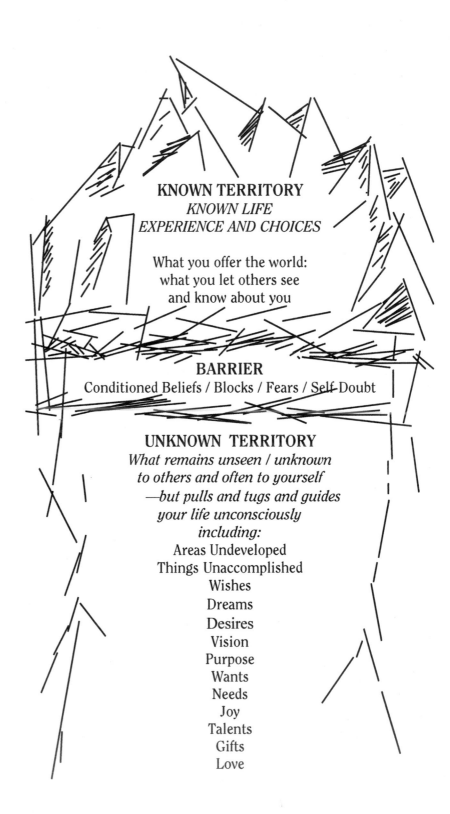

KNOWN TERRITORY
KNOWN LIFE
EXPERIENCE AND CHOICES

What you offer the world:
what you let others see
and know about you

BARRIER
Conditioned Beliefs / Blocks / Fears / Self-Doubt

UNKNOWN TERRITORY
What remains unseen / unknown
to others and often to yourself
—but pulls and tugs and guides
your life unconsciously
including:
Areas Undeveloped
Things Unaccomplished
Wishes
Dreams
Desires
Vision
Purpose
Wants
Needs
Joy
Talents
Gifts
Love

You must act as if it is
impossible to fail.

Ashanti proverb

Figure 11 The Iceberg

The "BARRIER" on the Iceberg, Figure 11 is water, dividing the everyday KNOWN LIFE from the UNKNOWN LIFE and potentialities. Water is the symbol for emotions! Of course, emotions. It is our emotions that fuel our thoughts that keep our greatest self, our gold and wealth of Self "submerged", down and away from our grasp. Without emotions our thoughts and ideas wouldn't go far before deflating.

TOUCHSTONE:
Without vigilance, fear is the strongest emotion.

EXERCISE:
Get out paper and pen and answer the following questions:

1. List those areas, talents, choices that are above the water in your life. What do you and others know about you? What have you risked to show, to create, to know? What do you hear yourself say when you exclaim, "I am . . . ."? This is what you believe is true about you.

2. What talents, gifts and abilities have you not used? What is still in the unknown? What do you think about often but dismiss as "crazy ideas" and "stupid"?

3. What is stopping you from using your talents and gifts?

4. Entertain the silence more often and listen to your thoughts about what you think is the truth about you. Is it true?

TOUCHSTONE:
Pay attention! When you say "I am..." you are announcing to the world, to the universe, to yourself what you claim as "the truth." Is that what and who you are? Is that what you want?

Many of us do not realize we have a problem because the way we live is a reflection of what we have lived with.

Iyanla Vanzant
Acts of Faith

To change one's life:
· Start immediately
· Do it flamboyantly
· No exceptions (no excuses).

William James

IV

---◦•●•◦---

Endings

---◦•●•◦---

We rarely see things for what they are.
Instead, we see the reflection of our own conditioning.
We believe and act on opinions and assumptions
as if they were reality, closing off other experiences.
. . . Old tapes create walls of many types.
Sometimes, just the conscious awareness of an old pattern is
enough to change the situation.
Other times, it is just a start.

Joan Borysenko
Minding the Body, Mending the Mind

All that we are arises with our thoughts.
With our thoughts, we make the world.

Buddha
(563-483 B.C.)

Chapter 9

STAGE 1: Beliefs

*Love of a new image of self leads to new knowledge
about oneself and one's potential.*

Thomas Moore
Care of the Soul

Deepak Chopra, in his ground breaking work, *Ageless Body, Timeless Mind*, speaks specifically about our mind-made limits regarding our mental model of aging and health. He says, "The impressions of past experience lock our minds into predictable patterns that trigger predictable behavior. Everyone's inner life is complex, swirling with both positive and negative thought patterns. But the fact that awareness can be trained, is simple, it is the most fundamental thing that happens to us from birth onward."[22]

EXERCISE:
Answer for yourself this list of questions:

- ❧ What beliefs (mindsets) keep you stuck, frustrated, limited and possibly living in your very own soap opera?
- ❧ Where did you get these beliefs?
- ❧ Whose beliefs are they?
- ❧ What keeps you from changing them?

TOUCHSTONE:
Just the verbal cues fed to us by our parents in early childhood, which continue to run throughout our lives on some level, amount to over *25,000 hours* of pure conditioning.[23]

CORE BELIEFS

Reexamining your mental models, conditioned beliefs, self-talk and identity must be a conscious process. To find the answers to the above questions, let's examine a list of Core Belief Areas that we each have.

Who I am.	The way the world is.
What I am.	The way my family is.
The way I am.	The way my culture is.
Who you are.	The way God is.
The way things are.	The way my ethnic group is.
How I lead my life.	The way relationships work.
The way I make decisions.	How my body is.
The way I live.	The way "they" are.
The way women are.	The way life is.
The way men are.	The way parents are.
My values.	The way my job is.
The way siblings are.	The way the government is.
The way children are.	The way I deal with emotions.
The way I am with money.	How I communicate.
The way I use my time.	The way my attitude is.
How I make choices.	The way "we" are.
The way society is.	The way it was.
The way it is.	The way it's going to be.
The way religion is.	My beliefs.

Thoughts are things; they have tremendous power. Thoughts crystallize into habit and habit solidifies into circumstances.

Brian Adams
How To Succeed

Each one of these beliefs, and more, is the first stage of the ReDecisions Model (Figure 12). This is where we like spending life—in Enlightenment, the known area—Who I Am. Here we believe that we know what's going on in our lives, who we are, how the world works. We feel in control, safe, secure and sometimes even self-righteous and smug in our "knowing the truth about things." All is well.

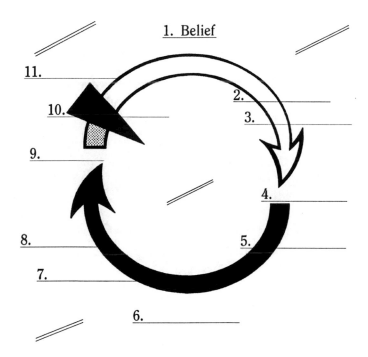

Figure 12 The ReDecisions 11-Stage Model - STAGE 1

EXERCISE:
Take time to reexamine each of these Core Belief Areas, defining them for yourself. What do you believe about each of them? What is your mindset, your mental model?

TOUCHSTONE:
Your life is directed and determined by every belief that you have.

As stated earlier, you were *taught* these areas of beliefs by parents, society, school, teachers, role models of many kinds, religion, cultural-ethnic background, the media and others. What you learned to be the facts, the truth, and the models and ideals to live life by as a child is how you are still living out your life today, unless you have taken time to reexamine your beliefs often. Are they working?

IDENTITY

At the beginning of one of my workshops I had each of the participants introduce themselves. A man stood up stating "I'm Pat. I'm a recovering alcoholic and a real sick puppy." I was aware of what Pat had said about himself, but didn't say anything at the time. Two months later, at another workshop, I asked participants to introduce themselves. Pat was attending again. He got up and introduced himself the same way. This time I stopped him. I asked Pat to introduce himself without negative, limiting labels. He said his name and his job title this time. He said he'd have to work on not using the other labels, that they'd become part of his thoughts, language and the world in which he lives—his identity.

Whatever we believe to be true, we live out. Whether good or bad, healthy or unhealthy, we live out our beliefs in our drama called Life. What we live out becomes our character, self-image, who we are, our Identity (Figure 13).

TOUCHSTONE:
Our thoughts and beliefs become our results, our reality, in life.

*You are searching for
the magic key
that will unlock the door
to the source of power;
and yet you have the key
in your own hands,
and you may use it
the moment you learn
to control your thoughts.*

Napoleon Hill
Think and Grow Rich

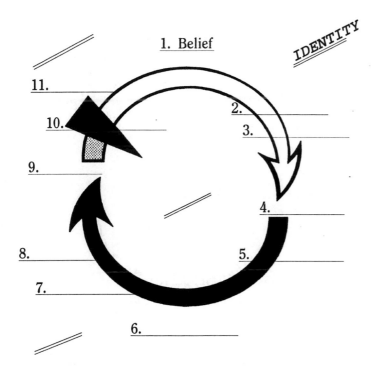

Figure 13 The ReDecisions 11-Stage Model - IDENTITY

Do you like who you are? Do you like the way your world is? If not, do you realize that you have total control over changing it? Do you realize that your beliefs may not be serving you?

Below is a list of some beliefs I've heard over the years from many different people from around the world. Can you relate to any of these statements?

- ❏ I've never been good at anything. I can't do it.
- ❏ I just don't think I can handle any more.
- ❏ I'm this way because my family is this way.
- ❏ I can't learn anything when it comes to (fill in the blank).
- ❏ I'm so tired and stressed out because (fill in the blank).
- ❏ I'm too old to change.
- ❏ I'm going to have (any illness or disease) because my parents had it.
- ❏ I'm this way because I grew up (race, religion, culture, country. . .).
- ❏ I wish I could have a better job, but I'll never be able to.
- ❏ I'm not smart enough.
- ❏ I'm not good-looking enough.

*You are given
the gifts of the gods;
you create your reality according
to your belief.
Yours is the creative energy that
makes your world.
There are no limitations
to the self
except those you believe in.*

Jane Roberts
The Nature of Personal Reality

- ❐ They (list whoever "they" are) are always that way.
- ❐ I've always struggled with money issues; I guess I always will.
- ❐ Relationships never work out for me.

And on they go. When people talk this way and think this way, about themselves, their lives and the world around them, they are living in beliefs that are limiting and self-sabotaging. They are also daily continuing to create and solidify an identity that greatly limits their perception, creativity, problem-solving and decision-making abilities.

WHAT IF?

The turning point question is: What if?

- ❧ What if my beliefs are not true?
- ❧ What if these statements of belief are wrong?
- ❧ And, if they are wrong, what changes?
- ❧ How would my life be different if I took every belief I have and challenged myself to look at it differently?

In other words, become a witness, an objective viewer, a mindful observer from the outside of your own life looking in.

TOUCHSTONE:
Beliefs create the limits for change.

BELIEF

Let's examine the word *belief* in order to reevaluate other mindsets. With a pen or pencil, cross off the first two letters and the last letter of the word below. What remains?

B E L I E F

"Oh!" Surprised? We must always be willing to realize that within every belief we have, no matter how "set" it is in our lives, there can be a *lie*, a non-truth, half-truth, falsehood. From Columbus' voyaging maps of a "flat world" to astronauts walking on the moon (they could never do that!) to 78-year-olds running marathons and graduating from high school and college, we have discovered over and over again that our beliefs can be wrong, they can limit us and that they, and ultimately we, can change.

> *As we let go of beliefs and belief systems, we can meet life directly, immediately, that is, without the mediation of concepts.*
>
> Ken Bear Hawk
> *Creation Spirituality Magazine*

> *If a thing is absolutely true, how can it not also be a life? An absolute must contain its opposite.*
>
> Charlotte Painter
> American writer and educator

If you're not sure about the fact that you have total control over your life, then perhaps it's important to understand how we examine our beliefs and how beliefs change.

EXERCISE:
Review again the list of Core Belief Areas on page 88. Reevaluate your patterned, conditioned and chosen thoughts and beliefs of each of them. Could there be some changes in your present belief system that could be upgraded for a more open, positive or healthy way of perception in any area?

The bottom line is, we must be *open and willing to question* our beliefs at all times, keeping us open and flexible to our changing world and changing needs.

WILLINGNESS

So, how is it that we come to a place of willingness to change our beliefs or to at least reevaluate and reconsider their validity and truth? How do we know when it's time to change, to grow?

In the next chapter we'll explore what it takes to evaluate and reconsider our beliefs, the need for change and, ultimately, personal transformation.

*When it comes time
to do your own life,
you either perpetuate your
childhood or you stand on it
and finally
kick it out from under.*

Rosellen Brown

*The life which is unexamined
is not worth living.*

Plato

There is nothing either good or bad,
but thinking makes it so.

William Shakespeare

Chapter 10

STAGE 2: The Event

*...the greater part of our happiness or misery
depends on our dispositions and not on our circumstances.*

Martha Washington (1731-1802)
First Lady

What does it take to get us to look at our beliefs differently and to think about changing them? Events (Figure 14).

Our change in perception and life transitions tend to begin with one, or both, of two events:

1. **Something happens from inside of us (*within* us).**
   We begin to experience a vague feeling of frustration, of feeling uncomfortable with our lives, relationships or jobs; or a mild to painful discontent that pushes us from the inside out to move, to question our decisions and life choices.

2. **Something happens from outside of us (*without* us).**
   We tend to say that these events happen "to us." Some classify them as wake-up calls. They might be in the form of an accident, a loss of some kind as in the death of a loved one or the loss of a job, or illness, or a divorce. There are many events that cause us to stop and look at our lives with new eyes.

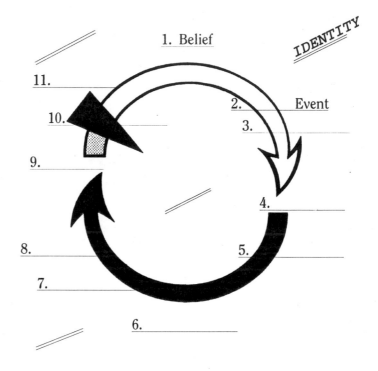

Figure 14 The ReDecisions 11-Stage Model - STAGE 2

*Change is never a loss -
it is change only.*

Vernon Howard
*The Mystic Path
to Cosmic Power*

Events are just events. Have you heard this said before? It's true. No matter what is happening in your life today, it is just happening. If what is happening wasn't happening, something else would be happening! Pretty simple, right? Then how is it that we can get so hooked and our buttons so pushed by sometimes seemingly small and insignificant events? These may be the same events that others don't even notice.

We jump and react because of—remember?—*patterned* or *conditioned responses*. It may also be called being *unconscious!* It is an unconscious, patterned response from childhood or some past experience that has turned into a conditioned "knee-jerk" fear reaction. Some psychotherapists have come to labeling this state of being on automatic a "trance" or "trance state" where one does things without even knowing it.

In her bestselling book, *Minding the Body, Mending the Mind*, Joan Borysenko, Ph.D. explains the process of conditioned habits, mindless repetition and programmed beliefs. "Human learning is a process of conditioning. Once a certain event has occurred, mental impressions are formed that favor its recurrence under similar circumstances. Remember Pavlov's dogs? Emotional events are conditioned in a similar fashion. Like old tapes, stored impressions can replay endlessly throughout life. This mindless repetition continues unless we shine the light of awareness on them and change our past conditioning—erase the worn-out tapes".[24]

So, the more conscious one becomes, by choosing to evaluate life events and manage the conditioned mindset reactionary response, the easier, less threatening and more enjoyable life becomes.

Sounds easy, right? Well, if you've read your daily newspaper or listened to the news lately, obviously it's not.

Figure 15

If the doors of perception were cleansed, man would see everything as it is, infinite.

William Blake

EXERCISE:
Above is a picture. What do you see? An old lady or a young lady? Do you see both? Do you see either?

Did it take you a while to see them both? Are you still not sure? If you're having a hard time seeing one or the other, or both, show it to several other people and listen for their ability to "see" the different pictures.

To "see" or "not to see" what is in front of us, to evaluate life's events more consciously, is related to our ability of perception. So, now that it has a label, how do you get there from here?

PERCEPTION

Suppose you go to the parking lot where your car is awaiting you after a long day at work. You notice that the car next to yours has a flat tire. An event—flat tire. You either acknowledge it and shrug it off, or you acknowledge it mentally and just think, "Hmm, they have a flat tire." You get into your car and drive away, putting this event out of your mind. It doesn't affect you.

Now, let's go through this scenario again. You leave work and go to the parking lot. This time it is *your car* that has a flat tire. An event—flat tire. What do you do? This is the critical point. Two responses are possible at this moment. Choice number 1 comes from conditioned response.   REACTIONARY PERCEPTION: "I can't believe this happened today. I don't have time for this. Why me?" And so on. This is black and white, reactionary, "awfulized" thinking, coming from a conditioned, unconscious response.

Choice number 2 is a conscious "action-ary" response. "ACTION-ARY" PERCEPTION: "Well, this is not great, but I'll deal with it. My options are...." Then positive action is taken to solve the problem and regain equilibrium.

Can you feel the difference?   Choice number 1 leads you in a downward spiral into anger, rage, confusion, fear and other out-of-control feelings, actions and drama. We do not think or act in an effective, focused or even rational manner. We truly "lose" ourselves. Some call this victim—martyr behavior —the "why me?" attitude.

Choice number 2 recognizes that "stuff happens" in life and that you have choices. It offers you a wide range of options to choose from to do something effective and realistic about the situation—to detach and decide your action. For example, I have what I call *Rent-A-Husband!* Knowing that I will have periodic car trouble, I have chosen to pay my membership fee each year for AAA service. If I lock myself out of my car, the battery goes dead, or a tire is flat, I don't have to get frustrated or lose my life energy over such a mundane event. I call AAA, they show up, fix the problem, I sign a form and I'm on my way. The event? A tire with no air on one side. That's it.

Here is another quick example of perception and events. It's a rainy July afternoon. A golfer is angry because her plans for teeing off are ruined, again. A few miles from the golfer, a farmer looks out over the land, grateful for the moisture that will help the crops grow. Is the

*Most of us bring
to everyday life
a somewhat naive
psychological attitude
in our expectations
that our lives
and relationships
will be simple.
Love of the soul asks for some
appreciation for its complexity.*

Thomas Moore
Care of the Soul

rain good or bad? Whose perception is right? Neither. Each has needs, wants and expectations that are affected by the event—water falling out of the sky. Whose perception may cause a ripple effect of emotional, physical and mental negative energy—upset—the rest of the day? Not the farmer's. So the issue doesn't stop with just the perception of the event. It continues with the person's conscious or unconscious response to the event.

If you have heard me speak, you have heard me say this statement often: "Life is very short." The sooner we "get" that events are just events, that whatever is happening, *is* happening, the sooner we will realize that events are always happening and always will, whether we're alive or dead. Learning to take a deep breath, to reexamine our options and control in the situation, and to recognize that our perception influences our choices is a very important ticket to inner freedom and calm on an ongoing basis.

TOUCHSTONE:
Happiness and peace are inside jobs.

WAKE-UP CALLS

Remember *Joe Versus the Volcano* and his "brain cloud"? Sometimes life events are wake-up calls, other times they are rude awakenings or even cosmic two-by-fours. Many events that jar us awake, into consciousness and transition, are those of loss or crisis: aging, illness, accidents, loss of jobs, divorce and the deaths of loved ones. One commonly discussed, and usually anguished, life event is called "mid-life crisis." Some see it as just that, a *crisis*, feeling helpless, frustrated and fearful, loathing every minute. Others see it differently. Their *perception* of this time of feeling off-center and confused is a mid-life *transition, adventure* or *quest*! It doesn't mean that they don't feel frustrated and sometimes scared, but they move away from fear and inaction and into choice more quickly, choosing to see the bigger picture. They get up in their "helicopter of life," look out over their life puzzle, reevaluate their life progress, choices and experiences to date and pro-actively make new choices for their future through a calmer, more focused process.

TOUCHSTONE:
Events are just events.

*Centuries-old belief systems
and behavior patterns
are disintegrating
as the rate of change
approaches the speed of light.*

Wes "Scoop" Nisker
Crazy Wisdom

CHANGE DICTATES CHANGE

Whether you perceive your life issues as an adventure or as a crisis, something that happened *within* or *without you*—"the way you've always done it" changes. You may find yourself packing up, leaving the big city and moving to the country. Or you may quit the travel-oriented, high-paying secure job and become self-employed, working more hours a week than you'd ever work for someone else, hopefully for more income, but sometimes less. The day comes where you finally say, "That's it...!" and you decide, or redecide, to let go and make some subtle (and sometimes not so subtle) life, work and relationship changes.

TOUCHSTONE:
If not now, when?

The average American life span in 1900 was 49 years; by 1990, it was 75. Due to improved living conditions and intense medical progress, we are living longer and healthier than ever before. From prehistoric times to the dawn of the Industrial Revolution, the average life span remained below 45; only 10 percent of the general population lived to age 65. But today, 80 percent of the population lives at least that long.[25]

Longer life spans provide more opportunities than ever before to make redecisions. Just think, people didn't live long enough to have mid-life crises before 1900!

In addition to living longer, technological advances and knowledge offer us many more opportunities for events to happen *in* our lives. A longer life offers us more opportunities to practice letting go— or holding on.

TOUCHSTONE:
Things don't happen *to* us. Things happen, and we happen to be a part of them at the time.

CHOICE

There are countless examples of events in any person's lifetime that can be perceived as good or bad, happy or sad, right or wrong. Events that will many times change the way one feels and perceives life forever. They can include illness, death of a lived one, job loss,

*I know that when
one door closes
another always opens...
but man,
these hallways are the pits!!*

Refrigerator magnet

birth of a child, winning an award, a suprise, gift or acknowledgment that made a difference, achievement of a challenging goal, and countless others. From experiences in war, to homeland terrorism, to the hieghts of falling in love and knowing success on any level, these events change our paths, our hearts and our minds.

Many people who have had tragedies befall them note that an event or wake-up call, though painful, helped to make them better people. Does this mean that illness, tragedy, pain and loss are good? No. *How you choose to deal with the event you experience is the challenge— your personal challenge.* In consciously facing the event, your thoughts, emotions and beliefs about it and yourself, you are challenging yourself to grow and respond to make proactive redecisions.

As long as you are alive, events of all kinds are going to happen in your life. How you choose to deal with them, perceive and respond to them is a part of your lifework to create character, grace and an attitude of moving through and overcoming life's dark side.

TOUCHSTONE:
Nothing holds more power over us than the beliefs held in our minds.

In order to experience life fully, we must not only adapt to change, but we must take a proactive role in it. We must be aware, conscious and willing to work with anything and everything that comes our way. We must be willing to take a mindful stand in taking charge of our mindset and perception of life events on an ongoing basis. And, because our perceptions are dramatically impacted by our overall mindset, we are responsible to keep a check and balance on our thoughts, attitude and life focus.

TOUCHSTONE:
No matter what happens in our lives, there is something we can learn from it.

We have little to no control over many circumstances in our lives. We do have control over our attitudes, how we perceive those circumstances and how we react or respond to the circumstances at each moment. This is always our individual responsibility.

EXERCISE:
Think of events that stirred a negative reaction in you this past week.
1. What was your belief (perception) about the event?
2. Can you change your negative perceptions of it in order to let go of the emotions that adversely affect you?
3. Can you choose to see it differently in order to be proactive?
4. What beliefs do you have that cause you frustration?
5. What *can* you do to change them?
6. What *will* you do to change them?

Anything you believe is changeable by altering your perception or your interpretation of what is happening or not happening. No matter how terrible the situation, you can change your world by changing your perception. Old programming limits you to old automatic perceptions. They are Default Programs, unconscious, like being on automatic pilot.

We will explore beliefs further in Stage 4.

STORY

A Zen Master was approached by one of his students asking why he was crying. The Master said that his infant son had died. The student considered this and said to his Master, "But you teach us that all of life is an illusion, that none of this is real. Why would you feel such great sadness?" The Zen Master answered, "Some illusions are more painful than others."

See every difficulty as a challenge, a stepping stone, and never be defeated by anything or anyone.

Eileen Caddy
The Dawn of Change

Chapter 11

STAGE 3: The Question

You cannot teach a man anything.
You can only help him discover it within himself.

Galileo Galilei
Astronomer and physicist (1564-1642)

❧

THE POWER OF FEAR

When negative or uncomfortable events happen, we tend to do three things. First, we get scared, second we complain and agonize a lot, which may include the act of blaming. Then hopefully, we Question (Figure 16) the event, our beliefs about it and how to deal with it.

As discussed earlier, many times we perceive events as fearful, threatening experiences. Something that has happened "to us" can leave us feeling out of control, fearful and angry. These feelings can cause us to close down, to shut off our peripheral vision, to become narrow-minded and stop any forward motion into workable answers and solutions.

EXERCISE:
Think of an event that is taking up a lot of your energy right now— one that causes you to react and feel out of control. With your right hand, palm up in front of you, visualize this event on the palm of your hand. Bring your hand up to your face and

rest the inside of your hand on your nose, restricting your eyesight. Move your head around so that you can look different places keeping your hand centered on your nose. How does this feel? Can you see?

Isn't this exactly what we do with fearful and threatening situations? They get so "in our face" that we literally can't "see" anything else. We lose perspective.

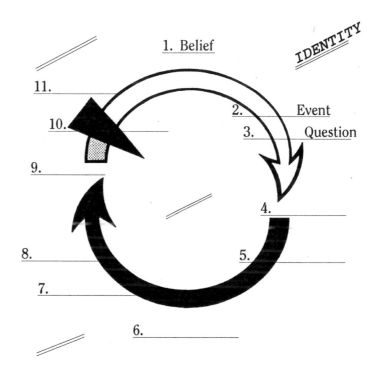

Figure 16   The ReDecisions 11-Stage Model - STAGE 3

Your questions indicate the depth of your belief. Look at the depth of your questions.

John & Lyn St. Clair Thomas
Eyes of the Beholder

TAKE CHARGE WITH EFFECTIVE QUESTIONS

There is another choice and that is to take charge of our thoughts. Taking charge of our thoughts, staying open, objective and conscious to options and choices that offer us positive, healthy ways to deal with the situation at hand is empowering. When we take charge of our thoughts and our actions, we are open to more than one way of looking at the event and solutions to resolve it.

As an educator, consultant and human being, I have found that people are always looking for *answers* to questions. Whether they are paying for this information or not, they are looking for someone to give them the answers or "permission" to do what they've really wanted to do anyway. Their history has taught them not to *trust themselves*. It is always a joy to watch someone "get it" when they learn to *ask the effective questions*, to risk living more fully.

TOUCHSTONE:
Learn to give yourself "permission"—to be, do and have different.

One of the requirements for asking the effective questions is consciousness. Most people walk, talk, work, play, live...unconsciously. Events happen and they *react*. They forget they have the power and freedom to detach and to live consciously and mindfully.

I've heard it said "I knew a person who died at 28, but he kept his body going way into his 60's." What dies? Our spirit, our soul. The event is the wake-up call, asking effective questions and being honest with ourselves assists us in a self-directed journey toward a positive turning point of choice and action. We have to take control over our minds, our thinking, to ask the questions.

As discussed in Chapter 10, at every moment we have total control over our minds, thoughts and actions regarding what we do in response to an event. We can easily find examples of unconscious behavior demonstrated in the media and all around us every day. These are examples of people *not* taking charge of their thoughts and choices—*reacting* to life events.

TOUCHSTONE:
Life is two-sided: loss and gain. There is always a price to pay.

LIFE: THE TWO-SIDED COIN
In order to become conscious in life, to deal more effectively with change of any kind, it is important to understand that there are two sides to every choice we make and to every event experience. Within every event there is loss and there is gain. No matter what the change is, joyful, sad or otherwise, there are two sides of the coin. The list below illustrates these two sides.

EVENT: *Marriage.*
    GAIN: Intimacy, partnership, sharing, love, nurturing.

We must be willing to get rid of the life we've planned, so as to have the life that is waiting for us. The old skin has to be shed before the new one can come. You can't make an omelet without breaking the eggs.

Joseph Campbell
A Joseph Campbell Companion

LOSS: Single life-style, freedom of time, personal choices, money choices.

EVENT: *Job promotion.*
GAIN: Increased income, title, network upgrade, travel options, benefits, perks.
LOSS: The way it used to be, old friends, and co-workers, time structure, less responsibilities.

EVENT: *Weight loss and body toning.*
GAIN: Feel good, look good, receive compliments.
LOSS: Security in the way you're used to your body and reactions from others, have to work on it consistently.

EVENT: *Financial freedom and money management.*
GAIN: More security in feeling in control and actual taking charge of life choices regarding money, higher self-esteem, self-confidence.
LOSS: Old identity of struggle, staying in a certain mindset of family and friends and "the way life is," may lose some family or friends who don't want to grow and change.

If we don't understand the gain and loss in every event, it is difficult to stay objective. Without objectivity, we react easily, losing our balance and our power to detach and to redecide.

TOUCHSTONE:
If you're alive, things will happen.
If you're dead, things will happen.

RESET BUTTONS

Because of their effect on our lives, there are several ways to stop and get a handle on the bigger picture of life when events throw us for a loop. These three techniques are like "reset" buttons, helping us to stop, "ground," "center" and "connect" with ourselves long enough to get some control over our situation. They help us regroup and get ready for proactive problem solving and decision making. These reset buttons are:

| Breathing | Anchoring | Reframing |

BREATHING

While reading the word *breathing*, did you find yourself consciously thinking about your breathing? Did you take a deep breath? It's amazing that we go moment by moment throughout our lives and never think much about our breathing process, the vital automatic process that literally keeps us alive.

TOUCHSTONE:
Your brain is hungry.

Have you fed your brain today? The brain is the organ with the greatest oxygen need in the body. Abdominal, or deep, breathing is one way to bring more oxygen fuel to your brain and relaxation to your body and mind.

Changing your breathing method can reduce or increase sympathetic nervous system activity, triggering either the fight-or-flight response or the relaxation response. Paying attention to your breathing is imperative as a reset button. Learning to notice your breathing pattern and being able to change it from tension-producing to relaxation-producing is one of the most crucial—and simplest—mind/body skills.[26]

So, when you are stressed and ready to *react* to an event, person, place or thing, STOP! BREATHE. Take five or ten seconds and just breathe *through* the feelings that usually accompany negative thoughts and fantasies about what happened or might happen. Stop the downward spiral in its tracks. Take charge of your mindset. Reset. And come from choice.

ANCHORING

Like the anchor of a ship that holds it in place in shifting, moving waters, there are *words, thoughts* or *sounds* that can do the same for you. There are several words and phrases that I've learned to use over the years to anchor my attention when my mind is racing, feels out of control or is unfocused. These include: "Let go," "Stop" and "Okay." Different people and different cultures have anchor words as well. In Switzerland, for example, after most sentences, they say, "So." Because it is an unconscious response, it is easy to pick up. After spending time there, I picked up the habit and use it now and again when I need to stop and reset. So!

I find that even when I'm in the events of shopping or doing office work, I can get overwhelmed with the many choices in the

Life has taught me to think, but thinking has not taught me to live.

Alexander Herzen
19th century
international journalist

computer store or the stacks of "have to do's" on my desk. The *Committee of the Mind* sets to arguing, nagging, condemning and a myriad of other feelings and thoughts. I can feel myself getting "out there," paralyzed with indecision. The mind-squirrel-wheel turns rapidly with no purpose. I have found that I can take simple action to stop the whirlwind and reset. I stop, take a deep breath in and sigh out, and say in my mind, and sometimes out loud, "Okay, now, what do I really need to do here?" Then I can feel anchored, grounded and centered again. I can jump back in to make more focused and realistic decisions. I take several of these reset breaths within seconds or minutes of each other depending on how off center I've become.

Find anchor words that work for you. Make sure, however, that the words you choose are not critical or devaluing to you. We each have had others in our lives who helped condition our mental response about ourselves in negative, put-down terms. These are not anchors. They are abusive and self-defeating. Find words that are neutral chatter stoppers like the ones noted above.

REFRAMING

When something happens, we can bring up the "computer screen of the mind." After viewing the various options and alternatives on the "menu," we can *reframe* it, see it differently and choose what action to take with a given event. It's kind of like rebooting a computer when the program gets frozen.

MIND WORKS

In order to use these three reset buttons, we have to become aware of the "computer screens of the mind" that we pull up to respond to events. These screens or programs include:
1. Reactionary Default Menu
2. "Action-ary" Response Menu
3. Pollyanna Menu.

The following is an example of an event and the different perceptions and questions that may accompany them from these different mindsets.

Nothing is so exhausting as indecision, and nothing is so futile.

Bertrand Russell

REACTIONARY MINDSET

EVENT: Your company is downsizing, and you always thought (old mindset) that you'd have a job "forever" with this company.

RESPONSE:

REACTIONARY DEFAULT MENU	
TOPIC:	**JOB LOSS**

Natural conditioned reaction
①   Why me?
②   Why is this happening now?
③   I hate this! I knew I shouldn't have trusted them.
④   How am I going to make a living? What will I do?

Can you feel the downward, out-of-control, fear-based belief system? This *reaction* can be very normal when something happens "out of the blue," or at least something we haven't been wanting to deal with and can't avoid any longer. This Reactionary Default Menu is also known as "awfulizing" and "catastrophizing." We default, automatically going back to the way we always deal with events. They are two myopic, limited ways of thinking, talking and behaving that add much color, drama and high blood pressure to our daily lives. They do create questions, however, the negative direction of the questions add little or no creative energy, health or positive focus.

EXERCISE:
Below are nine dots. With a pencil, connect all nine dots using four straight, continuous lines. The lines cannot curve. Your pencil must stay on the paper (you can't lift it up and make discontinuous lines).

    •   •   •

    •   •   •

    •   •   •

The answer to the nine dot exercise:

We have been conditioned to see this formation (the nine dots) as a box and four straight lines to usually mean "box." We *default* and go back to our only references to problem solve the issue. So, now what? There are always more ways to do something than what we've *always thought* was the *only way*. We must move *outside of the limits* of our perceptions and assumptions to understand how things work. Creativity demands the creative acts of problem solving and of stretching our limits. To keep your mind alert and flexible, the view of the bigger picture is always necessary.

TOUCHSTONE:
Always find the second right answer.

"ACTION-ARY" MINDSET

To change our conditioned response to life, we must take an active role to question our beliefs and learned responses on a continual basis. Effective questioning offers you the opportunity to pull up your "Action-ary" Response Menu. This menu offers options of awareness and consciousness, bringing up the bigger picture to make more objective choices.

Let's look at the same example of the event and the different perceptions and questions that accompany it from an *"action-ary" mindset*:

EVENT: Your company is downsizing, and you always thought (old mindset) that you'd have a job "forever" with this company.

RESPONSE:

"ACTION-ARY" RESPONSE MENU	
TOPIC:	**JOB LOSS**

Natural conditioned reaction
① Why me?
② Why is this happening now?
③ I hate this! I knew I shouldn't have trusted them.
④ How am I going to make a living? What will I do?

Take control over thoughts—turning point
❺ I hate this. But, *what if* it's time to look at all those things I wanted to do anyway. I never thought I'd leave here or ever get to do them.
❻ It feels scary and I'm feeling really frustrated right now. I know there are a lot of different things I can do.
❼ I look forward to finding out what's going on in the world.

Reset
❽ *Okay*. I'm going to make it. It may not be easy right away. But I know that I can make it.
❾ In fact, this might be a good thing! It's getting me out of a job that, even though I liked parts of it, I really wanted to try some new things. Sometimes I need this kind of push to move on.

Inner control taken
❿ I can handle it.

Can you feel the difference? Moving downward or upward on the spiral creates very different energies. How did it change? By shifting the mindset through effective questions.

WHAT IF?

The Default Program is the conditioned repetitive reaction to life. As noted earlier, by age 10, children learn everything they will know as it relates to how they will perceive the world, others and themselves for the rest of their lives. When any event or issue arises in life, at any age, most people *unconsciously* default, taking action from their childhood development. Why? Many people do not want to give up their old ways of reacting to life or have not been programmed or educated with an "Action-ary" Menu. Thus, an "Action-ary" Response Menu may not be available to them.

Being able to get "outside" the emotions of the moment and ask yourself a positive, proactive "What if...?" is a sure sign you are

*In the solitude of your mind are
the answers to all your questions
about life.
You must take the time
to ask and listen.*

Bawa Mahaiyaddeen

moving in the right direction. Number 5 in the "Action-ary" Response Menu is the transitional turning point out of the downward spiral into effective action-oriented questioning.

TOUCHSTONE:
There are reasons and results in life. And reasons don't count.

What if you don't have any positive "What if...?" questions to ask yourself? What if you don't have an "Action-ary" Response Menu? The only menu you've been running on for years has been the Reactionary Default Menu. Well, thank goodness for books, seminars, internet, television, radio, support groups, therapists, guidance counselors and healthy supportive friends and family. What a deal. You have "Action-ary" Menus to borrow from all around you.

TOUCHSTONE:
You are responsible for your actions. There are no excuses.

BEING THE STUDENT

Asking questions (letting go) to learn, unlearn and gain "input" for your "Action-ary" Response Menu will take a toll on your identity if you have an ego issue about this. "What will they think of me?" "They'll think I'm stupid because I don't already know how to deal with this situation," and so on. Remember, to hold on is to struggle.

TOUCHSTONE:
It is far better to be a student with sight than to be a teacher who is blind.

You must never be stupid enough to say, or smart enough to admit, you "know" what someone else is talking about. The moment you do your learning stops.

Awo Osun Kunle

One of the things I started doing to "get out of my own way" is to acknowledge that *I don't know what I don't know*. When I'm stuck and can't come up with effective questions or "Action-ary" Menu options, I simply explain to others, "I don't even know what questions to ask. Will you help me figure this out? Will you teach me?" Or, "Please educate me on this, I don't understand it. What do you think? I want to learn."

TOUCHSTONE:
Sometimes we don't know that we don't know.

As you ask many questions, you will get many answers. They may or may not work for you. Use the ones that work, let the rest go. And, as you continue to ask others and yourself more effective questions more often, you will find the answers coming from interesting places, including comic strips, songs, T-shirts, bumper stickers and from within yourself. This becomes the upward spiral, positive growth process in *trusting yourself.*

INNER AWAKENING

The "Action-ary" Response Menu promotes growth in a loop of consciousness that makes dealing with change, transition and life work more smoothly. This loop is a natural process that comes from questioning: *Awareness*, *Action* and *Actualization*. The more often we question ourselves, the more awareness we develop, the more effective action we will take and the more self-actualized we become.

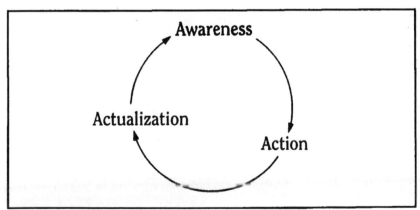

Figure 17 Awareness, Action, and Actualization

THE POLLYANNA MINDSET AND GRIEF

Is there ever a time when reframing and resetting is not healthy or helpful? Yes. I have worked with many people over the years who have had devastating events happen in their lives. Deaths of loved ones, terminal illnesses and other major losses. They tried to reframe these events *too quickly*. They pulled down the Pollyanna Menu.

*...sometimes I think
I'm just having
a near-life experience!!*

Ziggy
Tom Wilson, cartoonist

EVENT: Your company is downsizing, and you always thought (old mindset) that you'd have a job "forever" with this company.

RESPONSE:

POLLYANNA MENU
TOPIC: **JOB LOSS**

Natural conditioned reaction
① Why me?
② Why is this happening now?
③ I hate this! I knew I shouldn't have trusted them.
④ How am I going to make a living? What will I do?
Helpless, powerless reaction
❺ Well, this is the way life is to be. This is my fate.
❻ I must be strong and overcome my fears and emotions.
❼ There is no time to grieve, be angry or feel, just get on with life.
❽ I won't be weak. I won't cry.
❾ I need to be strong. It's my job. It's expected of me.
❿ This must be what God (whomever) wants for me.
   I must persevere.

The Pollyanna Menu might also be called the Victim, Martyr or Saint Menu. Although we may think we are letting go of the experience and floating through life, we may not have *grieved* the loss first. It's like putting a Band-Aid too quickly over an open wound without cleaning it and examining the needs of this specific injury. We have not let our minds and bodies work through the pain. Add some medication (legal or not) and/or alcohol and it's sure to boomerang.

The pain of loss and grief of any kind, if not dealt with appropriately, will sooner or later come out somewhere, usually *sideways*. Sideways looks like illness, anger, violence, isolation, depression, control, staying busy, even constant joking. In children we call this sideways behavior "acting out;" in adults, it is the same. Protective, defensive walls are put up to keep others away, so as to not get hurt again.

I've heard many people comment, "I don't get mad, I get even." As I've watched people reframe too quickly, not taking time to feel and heal their pain, it might be more correct to say, "I don't get mad, I got *perfect*." We get stronger, work harder, become nicer and take

*Don't be afraid to cry.
It will free your mind
of sorrowful thoughts.*

Hopi Indian saying

control even more than before. We keep stuffing our emotions and pain down and become more perfect, and more perfect, until...we blow or crack. It comes out sideways.

During times of loss, frustration and pain, grieve and deal with your feelings of being out-of-control. Feel your pain. Cry your tears. Take time out. Be kind and gentle with yourself. Reframe parts of the experience so that you can make objective decisions about what you need to do to get through it in one piece. Don't reframe the whole event too soon. Talk to others, share your experience, feelings and pain, seek professional help— you don't have to do it alone.

HAPPINESS AND SELF-ESTEEM

I would like to address one more kind of question before moving on from this Stage. This is the question regarding our right and choice to be happy. Yes, happy.

According to Nathaniel Brandon, in his book *The Six Pillars of Self-Esteem*, "Self-esteem is the disposition to experience oneself as competent to cope with the basic challenges of life and as worthy of happiness."[27] He talks about "happiness anxiety" as the courage to tolerate happiness without self-sabotage, without blocking and limiting our "right" to an enjoyable life experience.

Blocking our right to be happy shows up in various forms. Some people don't let themselves have nice things, "Oh, this is good enough"; some always buy for others before themselves, or give more than receive; still others don't let themselves enjoy relationships and the whole of life.

An unfortunate example and statistic of Default Programming regarding happiness and deservedness is that of battered women. A battered woman will go back to her abusive spouse or partner seven to eight times before leaving for good—alive or dead. Why? Programmed, conditioned learned response from childhood, low self-esteem and shallow to dry wells of conscious choices to pull from.

Most battered women, and men, grew up in homes where they were physically, sexually and/or emotionally abused by their fathers or other men, or at least witnessed their mothers and/or other women being abused. So, abuse, not letting oneself be happy, to these people's lives is "normal," it's automatic, history repeated. Sound strange? Look around you, at your friends, acquaintances and yourself. Notice patterns of behavior that seem unhealthy or a little uncomfortable, but continue because, well, "It's always been this

No one can make you feel inferior without your consent.

Eleanor Roosevelt
(1884-1962)

way." "This is just the way it is." Or it is so unconscious that it is not questioned at all. No one even notices.

The story about a frog that was put into a pan of boiling water illustrates this well. When he hit the scalding water he immediately jumped out. The pain was too great. He saved himself. The same frog was put into a pan of cool water. He sat there quite content. The burner on the stove was turned on, and the water became lukewarm, hot, then boiling. As did the frog. Why didn't he jump out? Why didn't he save himself? Because the change, the conditioning of the water, was gradual. He got used to it. He was unconscious of the change and the condition.

EXERCISE:
Think of a situation you are dealing with presently to which you can apply the two program menus: Reactionary Default Menu and "Action-ary" Response Menu.

1. What Reactionary Menu items are you choosing that are creating increased frustration and stress?

2. What "Action-ary" Menu items can you choose in order to be more objective about the situation and literally give yourself room to breathe?

Take time to write out the issue you are dealing with and the options, reactive or active, that you can think of. Ask others for input if you can't seem to think of options. Evaluate your lists and make the most effective choices you can.

The following is a quick overview of this chapter's information—a simple guide, with workable steps to a more fulfilling life.

People create their own questions because they're afraid to look straight.
All you have to do is look straight and see the road, and when you see it,
don't sit looking at it—walk.

Ayn Rand

SIX KEYS TO BEING IN CHARGE OF YOUR LIFE

1. STOP—*BREATHE,*
   Reset.

2. BECOME *AWARE,*
   Be conscious.

3. *THINK* THROUGH THE SITUATION,
   Challenge yourself.

4. COME FROM *CHOICE,*
   Effectively choose from a broader base of options.

5. TAKE FOCUSED *ACTION,*
   Move and change.

6. LET GO,
   Stop scaring yourself. Grow.

*Know thy ideal
and live for that.
For each soul must give an
account for its own self.*

Paramhansa Yogananda

Let me not pray to be sheltered from dangers
but to be fearless in facing them.
Let me not beg for the stilling of my pain
but for the heart to conquer it.

Rabindranath Tagore
A Prayer

Chapter 12

STAGE 4: Transition

*Care of the soul...appreciates the mystery of human suffering and
does not offer the illusion of the problem-free life.
It sees every fall into ignorance and confusion
as an opportunity to discover that
the beast residing at the center of the labyrinth
is also an angel.
The uniqueness of a person is made up of
the insane and the twisted
as much as it is of the rational and normal.*

Thomas Moore
Care of the Soul

THE PUZZLE

Our original Belief, Stage 1, is like a puzzle. All the pieces are there
and fit. We know the picture, but whether we know how it really all
fits together is not usually questioned until something happens to
shake up a persons world, routine or process. Remember, the Event
can be postive, negative, big or small. The bottom-line is that it
changes the "way it's always been", changing it just a little, to blowing
the puzzle apart, scattering it to pieces.

The Questioning Stage looks at all the puzzle pieces and tries to fit
them back together. If it's time to change, to grow, the pieces won't
fit the same again. New pieces will be added. Some old pieces will be
discarded. The picture has to change. We begin our journey out of
the comfort zone into Transition (Figure 18).

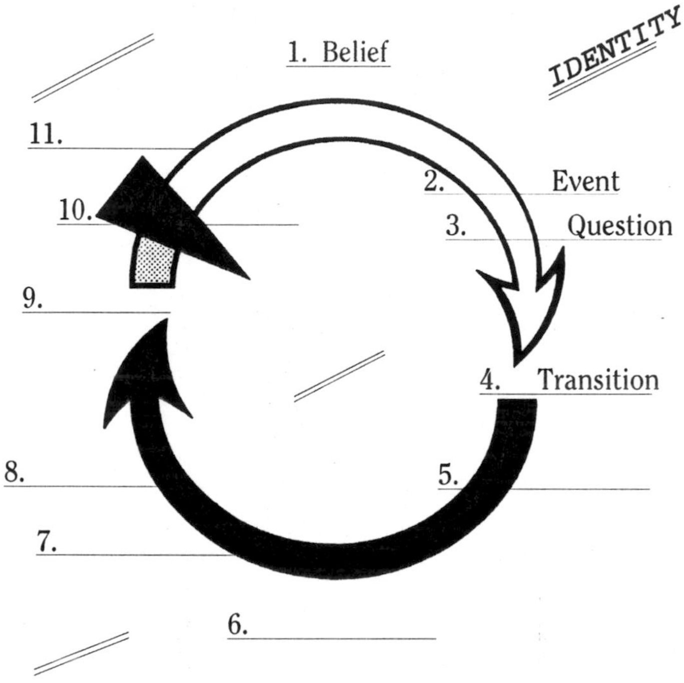

Figure 18 The ReDecisions 11-Stage Model - STAGE 4

Sometimes there is not a clear
moment when the fall begins;
there is just a thickening
of life's energy,
as if a person had been sleeping
on a hillside,
and awoke to find the
weather changed,
the landscape unfamiliar,
and wild beasts approaching.
That is Dante's story,
and it is common in a life
that is otherwise peaceful.

John Tarrant
The Light Inside the Dark

RISK-TAKING

To reconsider our beliefs is risk-taking. It sets us up for change and transition. We begin to identify with Dorothy upon landing in OZ: "Toto. I have a feeling we're not in Kansas anymore."

We tend to move into the Transition Stage with little grace. The journey toward deeper understanding and a higher level of maturity moves us into Endarkenment—that area of life where it feels dark, gray, murky and uneasy. It can feel unsafe, insecure, overwhelming and even threatening. Feeling out of control can develop reactions of immature and out-of-character behavior that surprise even us.

What we believed was true is now up for debate, and we are off solid ground. Confusion, anxiety and apprehension are normal. We may hear, "I don't know..." a lot at this stage.

DRAGONS AND MONSTERS

Solid beliefs that we fight to hold on to, against questions for change and especially a move into transition, are like the maps from the Middle Ages. These maps were beautifully created, usually seen on parchment paper, with scrolled or burnt edges. There is the "Land of the Known," where we are safe and in fact *know everything*. Then there is *beyond* the edge of the known, the "Land Where Dragons Live."

Figure 19 Map of the Known and Unknown

Aren't these wonderful maps? We know today that none of this is true. Remember the exercise of crossing out the BE and F of belief? It's a LIE. There are no dragons. There never were. There were only people, places and things that were not yet discovered—by people who had not yet been there, as opposed to the people who already lived there and didn't know that they were unknown and needed to be discovered!

What and who are your monsters and dragons? What and who do you point at to blame for your life's frustrations, blocks and fears? Isn't this exactly the way many people live in the world today, this moment? You hear it all the time.

"I'm afraid to try (it), what if *they* (the dragons) don't like it?"
"What if (it) doesn't work (and the dragons eat me)?"
"What if (they) don't like me?"
"What if (they) get angry with me?"
"What if (they) leave me or stop loving me?"

And so on.

Giving your power away to the dragons is a conditioned pattern. And, for most people, a lifetime of giving up one's power creates years of frustration and feelings of helplessness, hopelessness, anger and regret. Living with feelings of regret sound like blame, criticism and resentment.

"It's all (their) fault."
"If (they) wouldn't have (fill in)."
"If (they) would have (fill in), then (fill in)."

TOUCHSTONE:
You are your responsibility.

Learning to *dance with your dragons*, instead of *feeding* them with fear, is an interesting and wonderful adventure! Daring yourself to risk to try new things, to go beyond "the way it's always been," challenges your conditioned beliefs, your fears and your identity. In essence, it challenges you to embrace your dragons.

EXERCISE:
Determine where your dragons and monsters live, who and what they are—stopping you from claiming your holy grail. Complete the following sentences:

Every issue, belief, attitude or assumption is precisely the isssue that stands between you and your relationships to another human being; and between you and yourself.

Gita Bellin

1. I wish . . ., but . . . .
2. I'd really like to . . ., but . . . .
3. I would . . ., but . . . .
4. My life would be happier if . . . .
5. I want to . . ., but . . . .

I will expand on the issues of fear, doubt, risk and moving beyond the "Known Territory," in Chapter 14 on Doubt and Fear.

TOUCHSTONE:
Stop feeding the dragons!

To attain the deepest spirituality, no emotion need be denied: pleasure, anguish, desire, and contentment all form a part of the soul's great quest.

John Tarrant
The Light Inside the Dark

What we are today comes from our thoughts of yesterday, and our present thoughts build our life of tomorrow: Our life is the creation of our mind.

The Buddha

V

---•◦●◦•---

The Void

---•◦●◦•---

Dark nights of the soul are extended periods of dwelling
at the threshold when it seems as if we can no longer
trust the very ground we stand on,
when there is nothing familiar left
to hold onto that can give us comfort.
If we have a strong belief
that our suffering is in the service of growth,
dark night experiences can lead us to
depth of psychological and spiritual healing and revelation
that we literally could not have dreamed of
that are difficult to describe in words without sounding trite.

Joan Borysenko
Fire in the Soul

> *One learns in life to keep silent*
> *and to draw one's own confusions.*
>
> Cornelia Otis Skinner
> American actress and author
> (1901-1979)

Chapter 13

STAGE 5: Confusion

See, the human mind is kind of like... a piñata.
When it breaks open,
there's a lot of surprises inside.
Once you get the piñata perspective,
you see that losing your mind
can be a peak experience.

Jane Wagner
The Search for Signs of Intelligent Life in the Universe

❧

You might literally hear yourself say, "I'm confused." "I don't get it anymore." "This doesn't make sense." Confusion leads to even more questions and conversations of inquiry with others to try to make sense of what is happening (Figure 20).

LEARNED LIMITATION

To illustrate conditioned behavior and its power over our thinking, acting and life movement, let's consider a fish story. An aquarium was set up and, as is normal, the fish swam throughout the tank, using up the entire space. Then researchers divided the tank of water down the middle with a sheet of glass. The fish could now only swim on one side of the tank. After a time, the divider was removed from the tank, but the fish continued swimming only on one half of the tank.

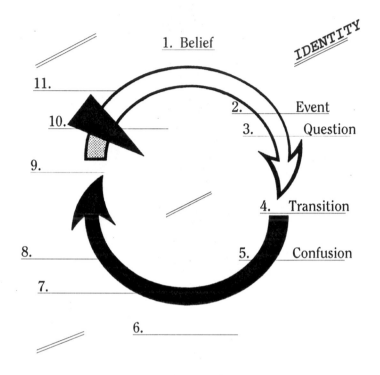

Figure 20 The ReDecisions 11-Stage Model - STAGE 5

TOUCHSTONE:
What you believe is true can limit you from the truth.

Several years ago, I met Mary at one of my workshops. She had been writing a novel for years and talked about it often. I didn't know much about writing or publishing at the time, but I asked my friend Joan, who has had many books published, if she would consider giving Mary's novel a look to see if it had any merit. She agreed. After reading the chapters Mary sent her, Joan responded with great support for the novel. She said she thought it would do very well and to get the rest to her soon, that she would get it on to her publisher.

Wow. What a deal. Mary could realize her dream: her novel in print. I told Mary about Joan's invitation to move her book along. To my great surprise and confusion, Mary said, "No. I won't be publishing it." Mary refused to follow through. Her fear was that "if they really like it, and it does well, they might want another book from me. And I don't know if I have another book in me."

Fear of success, fear of acknowledgment, fear of growth. Mary had reasons for her fears—a childhood of real life and death war-time drama and trauma in another country. She was kept quiet, hidden in closets and car trunks so that "she and her family wouldn't be caught." Now, like the great white elephant who was only running from her own fear, Mary is hiding and limiting herself. There's no one "out there" any more.

The power of conditioned learning is amazing. Each of us has similar conditioning from childhood, now patterned, unconscious thoughts and behaviors. And like the fish in the tank, we live our lives only half as much as is possible.

*Reality is
the leading cause of stress
amongst those in touch with it.*

Jane Wagner

TOUCHSTONE:
It is said that if you live with self-deceptions long enough, you become what you believe.

LOYALTY
The confusion comes from questioning our old belief. It's almost like a disloyalty to ourselves or to what was right—like breaking "the rules."

I have often listened to conversations that sound like this:
  "I'd really like to . . . .."
    "Why don't you try it?"
  "Oh, I couldn't."
    "Why not?"
  "Oh, I just couldn't, because . . . .."

The "because" supplies rationale that is not rational. But it makes a good brick wall.

TOUCHSTONE:
Not everyone is going to like your changes and growth.
Everyone doesn't have to.

This confusion can leave us feeling guilty or fearful of someone finding out or confronting us on why we've "stepped out of line." Yes, there will be those who don't like our changes and new beliefs. Some will understand and welcome the changes. They may even agree, "It's about time!" Others will ask you what's wrong with you or "What do you think you're doing?"

THE RIPPLE EFFECT

Each of us are a part of the whole. We don't do anything "all alone." Others will always be affected by our changes, whether they are positive or negative. Some people in your life may not like that your new direction is actually good for you. Though they may not like it, you are responsible to communicate your needs and changes to your immediate family and others you share your life with. It's not okay to surprise them with major changes that affect them, too.

The following story is a good analogy of our life changes and their effects on others. You walk along a beach where a fisherperson (that's politically correct!) is fishing for crabs. You notice that the bucket in which the crabs are kept doesn't have a lid. The crabs would seem to be able to just crawl out and walk back into the sea, free little creatures, at will. However, if you watch them in that bucket, you will understand why they end up on the dinner table. As one of the little guys crawls to the top of the bucket on the backs of others, only a claw's flip away from freedom, something happens. The other crabs start to pull him back in, trying to crawl on top of him to get out, and on it goes. No one escapes.

Have you ever experienced this in your life? As you move from the Questioning to the Confusion Stage, asking questions of family, friends and co-workers that may make THEM uncomfortable (their shadow issues), they may unconsciously try to pull you back into the bucket—the place where they are. The place where, well, "isn't everyone?" Because if you grow and change and, in fact, succeed, then it certainly is a reflection on everyone around you that they could, too. They may not want to grow and so resist the new consciousness that would take them through major identity changes—the stages you are experiencing.

TOUCHSTONE:
Stay away from "bucket people."

One of my workshop participants in South Dakota relayed a painful and tragic example of this. He worked for social services and said that just a few months prior to that workshop a teenage boy in a Midwest town was shot by several of his classmates from the same school. The reason? The victim was doing well in school. He had grown up

The confusion is not my invention....
It is all around us and our only chance is to let it in.
The only chance of renovation is to open our eyes and see the mess....

Samuel Beckett

around the other boys and, after working very hard, was getting A's and high B's in all of his classes. His teachers gave him much support and people liked him. He was successful. The classmates who killed him reasoned that he was making them look bad due to his positive lifestyle. They had to "get rid of him" so that *they* didn't have to change.

The mind is a tool we use;
it is not meant to be our jailer.

Joan Borysenko
Minding the Body,
Mending the Mind

EXERCISE:
Think about the following questions and write the answers down.

1. Who pulls you back into the bucket?
2. Who stops you from growing, changing, living?
3. How do they do this?
4. How do you let them?
5. What can you do about it?
6. What will you do about it?

MINDSET DEVELOPMENT

TOUCHSTONE:
Belief systems, positive and negative, are learned and grown.

What are the loyalties and beliefs that come to the surface in our confusion? The following is a list of negative or limited thoughts and statements many of us have incorporated into our identities.

CONDITIONING STATEMENTS

Don't be selfish.
Make us proud of you.
Keep in control.
Be perfect.
Be polite.
Don't be a child.
Be strong.
Be nice.
Don't be afraid.
Don't be.
Don't think.
Try harder.
Can't you do anything right?
Don't make it.
Don't belong.
Be clean.
Don't let your emotions show.
Don't grow up.
Don't cry.
Don't laugh.
Don't be angry.
Don't fight back.
Grit your teeth and bear it.
Don't be sad.
Don't be hurt.
Don't be happy.
Don't interrupt.
Don't talk too much.
Don't be so smart.
Don't brag.
Don't be important.
Don't be close.
Don't touch.
Children should be seen and not heard.

What will other people think?
You're not smart enough.
Oh, just forget it, give it to me.
Don't talk back.
Get off your high horse.
Don't feel (don't feel that).
Don't make trouble.
Don't rock the boat.
Be careful or you might get hurt.
You're not pretty enough.
You're not good enough.
You were a mistake.
You are a mistake.
You're no good.
You should have been a boy.
You should have been a girl.
You should be like (someone else).
You're not athletic.
You can't learn math.
You're too old for....
You're too young for....
You'd be okay if....
What's wrong with you?
Quit acting that way.
Girls don't....
Boys don't....
In our family we don't....
Don't ask stupid questions.
Don't speak your mind.
If you can't say anything nice,
Don't say anything at all.
"We"know better than you.
Who do you think you are?

Reaching the soul's own material
is an achievement.
When we begin the work by
beginning to fall,
we have little awareness
of the foundation.
It is bedrock,
and we must be stripped down
before we can arrive at it.

John Tarrant
The Light Inside the Dark

Now, add cursing, high voltage anger to this, maybe some alcohol or over-medicating and you've got a recipe for conditioning stuck deep in the cells.

Do you have a few to add to the list? In growing up, what messages have you heard or received that are not listed above?

EXERCISE:
Choose three messages from the list (or others that are not listed) and identify their ramifications in your life. List how they have affected your adult thinking, behavior and life choices.

Even though you may be able to read through this list and think, "Geez, how can people think this way?" you have your own list that controls and directs your life as well. Even if your list only had one of these, it can affect your life like a domino system. Everything is colored by your beliefs, good or bad. They are the filter through which you view everything.

Peggy, a workshop participant, told of how as an only child, she never saw or heard her parents fight. They either went into another room or just didn't argue in front of her. This might seem like a good thing considering all of the blaming we hear of parents being abusive, violent, and combative. However, as an adult, Peggy found that she doesn't know how to deal with anger—her own or others'. She doesn't know how to deal with confrontation. Where would she have learned? What she did learn was how to be "nice" to everyone all the time. It shows up "sideways" in her body as stress related illnesses and reactions due to the fear of dealing with any negative situation with others. Peggy decided to invest in some short-term counseling to help her "learn how to fight" and to deal with confrontation in a positive, healthy way.

Yea, though I walk through the valley of the shadow of death, I will fear no evil for thou art with me.

Psalm 23:4
The Bible

Loyalty to any belief that is limiting you will cause you pain and confusion sooner or later. Openness to change and questioning will keep you flexible and a lot less stressed.

BOXES
Because as human beings we like things categorized, filed, labeled and in boxes, the Confusion Stage tends to be very uncomfortable. Confusion comes from the struggle between the old belief—Known Territory—and the new beliefs—Unknown Territory—that remain foggy and unclear.

I hear people in this stage say, "Man, I hate this. I just wish everything was back to normal." "If I could just get a handle on this, I'd be all right." "If I could just figure it out and get back to the way it was." "If I could just get it over with." We want answers, we want boxes, we want to feel comfortable, safe and secure again.

Depending on the belief that is being questioned, the transition process may take minutes or it may take years. Another factor is how much true conscious energy we are willing to put into the process. It is also about being open and willing to let go, to change and to understand that the answers to our questions may be different than what we expected or wished.

Although it feels uncomfortable, really *awful* sometimes, confusion, like all other emotions, is not a bad thing, it just is. It is an event within the process taking place within you. It is a necessary part of the redecision and growth process. It is a time of wandering aimlessly *inside* ourselves, looking for answers to sometimes foggy, nonverbalized questions. Feeling lost and disconnected is the period of letting go of ego and the known, to further our transition into our greater Self.

There ain't no answer.
There ain't going to be
any answer.
There never has been an answer.
That's the answer.

Gertrude Stein

Chapter 14

STAGE 6: Doubt and Fear

Fear not.
What is not real, never was and never will be.
What is real, always was and cannot be destroyed.

Bhagavad Gita

THE DARK NIGHT OF THE SOUL

When we question our beliefs and set up a momentum for change, we may find doors open with an invitation to new choices. We may also find doors closed or hard to find. It's not uncommon for us to feel scared, frustrated, confused and sometimes numb and hopeless. We all go through this process many times in our lives. These times of doubt and fear, emptiness and meaninglessness, have been felt and struggled with for centuries. The great Spanish mystic, St. John of the Cross (1542-1591), wrote intensely about this experience, calling it "the dark night of the soul." This time of feeling stuck in Doubt and Fear (Figure 21) has also been called the underworld and death. The death side of the cycle takes us out of the *light* of our solid belief, where we *know who we are* and how *it* works. Everything shifts—we move down into the dark.

Dark nights of the soul are extended periods of dwelling at the threshold when it seems as if we can no longer trust the very ground we stand on, when there is nothing familiar left to hold onto that can give us comfort.[28]

Like letting go of the side of the swimming pool when taking your first swimming lessons, there is much doubt and fear that you will really float, no matter what the other swimmers are doing or what your instructor says will work. It's scary letting go of the side of the pool, stable ground, Known Territory.

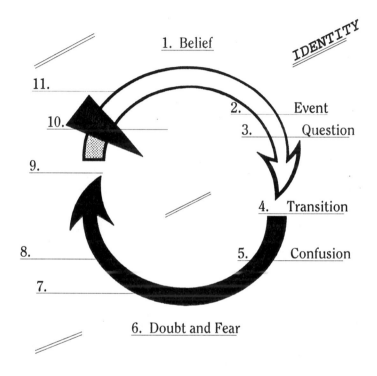

Figure 21 The ReDecisions 11-Stage Model - STAGE 6

TOUCHSTONE:
Fear will never go away as long as you are alive and continue to grow.

*And the earth was without form,
and void;
and darkness was upon
the face of the deep.*

*Genesis 1:2
The Bible*

LOSS AND GRIEF

No matter the size or degree of change we experience, there is always too a degree of loss—loss of your belief, what you knew was "normal" and your way of life. And, in any loss, there is a measure of grief.

As I discussed in Chapter 11 about reframing, it is important in this Stage as well to be aware of *not* reframing *too soon.* Depending on the severity of the loss or change, there may be minutes, days, even years of letting go and grieving the loss itself and letting go of an old mindset or belief that holds the attachment.

For most people there is a pattern to grief. The following 11 stages are part of the pattern. You may go through each of these stages in succession, skip some or jump back and forth between them during your process.

1. Shock/Denial
2. Facing emotions: anger, fear
3. Bargaining
4. Depression/Loneliness
5. Physical symptoms
6. Panic
7. Guilt
8. Hostility/Resentment
9. Drifting/Inability to return to usual activities
10. Acceptance/Hope
11. Reaffirmation of reality

As indicated above, the time it takes to work through painful events may also be tied up in denial. Denying the situation only holds it in place. It will have to be dealt with sometime. My friend Lori illustrates the denial Pollyanna Menu best with the reframing process of some people she knows. She says, "It's like people are thinking, 'It's not hot. This is not hell. And I'm not here.' Well, it is and you are! Sorry. Deal with it!"[29]

FEELINGS

The process of doubt and fear doesn't feel good, it hurts. The Pollyanna Menu, Chapter 11, will not serve you to move *through* this Stage but only to go around it, to avoid fear and doubt. Sooner or later your inner "nagging" will demand that you pay attention and face the changes needed, which ultimately means letting go and *feeling* your emotions.

Feeling anger, a natural part of the grief process, can also be a part of this Stage due to the conscious awareness of what is *not* changing. The transition is not happening the way you want it and usually not fast enough. Have you ever found yourself feeling frustrated that "it" won't just move on or change already? Feeling like you're in a struggle with quicksand? It is easy to get short-tempered with ourselves and with what my friend Lisa calls the "P" word—Process.[30] We just want to get on with it already. We want to *know* the answers and feel balanced, assured that we're on steady ground again. We're tired of thinking, feeling and *processing* the feelings, thoughts and

The ascent to the bright peaks of true being is always preceded by a direct descent into the dark depths. Only if we venture repeatedly through zones of annihilation can our contact with Divine Being, which is beyond annihilation, become firm and stable.

Karlfried Graf von Dürckheim
Daily Life as Spiritual Exercise

images in our minds. We're tired of confusion and feeling lost in a fog.

TOUCHSTONE:
We don't always have complete control over the timing of the process we're going through nor the length of our lesson.

Depression, then, can also become a part of the Doubt and Fear Stage. Mild or extreme, the feeling of depression can keep us off balance, disconnected and scared, sometimes taking us down further than we've ever felt possible.

Feeling sad, lonely, lost, numb and that "life is meaningless" are just a few of the aspects of depression. "I don't even care any more" and "I don't know. Whatever," may be what we hear ourselves think and say to others about where we are.

TOUCHSTONE:
Nothing lasts forever.

In therapy and recovery work, this is called "hitting your bottom." The bottom, or the "void," is when we can't use our logical, linear thinking minds to "fix" ourselves out of our situation. We are at the mercy of the unseen and unknown. Our prayers seem unanswered, and everything feels dark and heavy. We can feel empty.

STRUGGLE

Doubt and Fear is one of the hardest stages to move through. Some people stay struggling in it for moments, others for long periods of time. Some spend their entire lives in struggle.

TOUCHSTONE:
Whatever you resist you expand and pull toward you.

When we know we are being asked, from within and without, to change and to grow, and *don't* take the necessary steps to fulfill this guidance, we struggle. We create our own suffering at this point due to holding on, attachment.

Those who don't know how to weep with their whole heart, don't know how to laugh either.

Golda Meir

A phrase comes to mind regarding our holding on beliefs and our life process: *We are not human beings having a spiritual experience, we are spiritual beings having a human experience.* We are struggling between our "false self," the conditioned belief, the mindset that said we were a certain way, and our "true Self," that more conscious, honest, whole (and holy) person we are *always* in the process of "becoming."

TOUCHSTONE:
No one keeps us stuck. We do it to ourselves.

BEING EMPTY
When we get to the point of "I don't know" we are empty. We let go, detach, and are open to be *filled up* with answers. This is a very important shift.

Buddhist teachings are helpful in showing us how to work with our struggle and feelings of emptiness, loss and fear during this time. "Right action" is an approach to finding hope in times of adversity, a way of behaving that helps one weave and flow with the darkness. Rather than pushing and shoving, demanding that the issue be resolved, the Buddhist approach is one of openness, an attitude of the mindset I discussed earlier —"don't know." "Don't know" allows for stillness, for openness and for wisdom. From this perspective, hope for change and regrounding is not at all the future wish but a *depth of understanding* that can transform perception, past and future, as well as lead to conscious action that helps to shape future events. It is the ultimate in letting go of our way of "fixing" our situation. There is a lesson of trust and faith in this letting go to "I don't know."

If we cannot get to "I don't know," we are holding on, attaching, which keeps us stuck. We are hurting ourselves. The old belief doesn't work any more.

TOUCHSTONE:
Let go of trying to know the unknowable.

We can also *keep* from being empty by manipulating time and energy with useless activity that keeps us from ourselves. Examples of this might be leaving the television running when no one is watching it; leaving the radio and other noise on when others are trying to talk with you; cleaning, arranging and moving your living space around

Your pain is the breaking of the shell that encloses your understanding.

Kahlil Gibran
The Prophet

A thing is complete when you can let it be.

Gita Bellin

when it's not necessary; or talking on the phone to escape time and thoughts. Truly ineffective and unhealthy deterrents are the use and abuse of alcohol, drugs, food and other addictive substances and compulsive behaviors like shopping and spending money. These activities and behaviors are counterproductive. They not only keep us from ourselves, but they can develop into out-of-control habits that only make the doubt and fear more painful than need be.

Remember my story about my *swimming* out into the ocean? Let go and flow! I'm still not a water person, but I got the lesson: Life Lesson #504—let go of control.

❧

TOUCHSTONE:
Trust the natural process of things.

WHY ME?

Conditioned beliefs and attitudes come from many places in our lives effecting our ability and openness to change and deal with painful events. In her book, *Fire in the Soul*, Joan Borysenko explores how a person's attitude and religious conditioning toward illness affects their wellness and how we deal with diversity, pain and crisis, the dark night. She notes that psychologists classify people as optimists or pessimists based on how they answer the question "Why me?" The pessimist, a person with a victim mentality, believes: It's all my fault, it's the story of my life and I mess up everything I do. The optimist believes: *Life's challenges are part of your psychological and spiritual growth, expected and to be lived through.*[31]

Research shows that if people have a strong belief that their *suffering is in the service of growth*, dark night experiences can lead them to depths of psychological and spiritual healing and revelation that they literally could not have dreamed of.[32] Not that it's important to find a reason for everything that happens in our lives, as that can lead to premature reframing of the situation and detaching too soon. But, it is important to view the experience from an objective, detached, *witnessing* stance to see what you *can* reap from it and take back "up" with you when you emerge from this painful place.

The Stage of Doubt and Fear is a time to be still. It's time to listen for and to the "still, small voice." Through blind faith, stop the struggle. Sit still. Breathe. Just be.

Some days...it feels like all I'm doing is rearranging deck chairs on the Titanic!

Refrigerator magnet

I'm tired of blessings in disguise; If it's all the same to you, I want one I can recognize immediately!

Frank and Ernest
Bob Thaves, cartoonist

EXERCISE:
Think about a "dark night of the soul" that you have experienced.

❧   How did you deal with fear and doubt?

If you are in fear and doubt now about some issue, write down what old belief this transition is dealing with.

1.   What does this loss, change or transition mean to you?
2.   What are you being asked to let go of?
3.   What do you fear will happen if you let go of it?
4.   Is your fear valid, is it true?
5.   What if . . . your fear is not true?
6.   What can you do toward letting go?

Every substantial grief has twenty shadows and most of the shadows are of your own making.

Sydney Smith

PRAYER

To move through the Stage of Doubt and Fear, we must at some point realize that our human/ego, mind/body control will not change the situation. We must let go in order to gain the answers. We begin to accept our situation, surrender to whatever the change may be and to let go of the struggle. We may not know exactly what the answer is, but we open ourselves to trust that the answer will come. We start seeing a few puzzle pieces of the "new way," and we begin to evaluate our options, fitting together these new pieces for the new picture— the new belief.

There is an age-old story told about a man named Harry. All of his life Harry had wanted to climb one great mountain. One day, he decided it was time. He climbed all day and upon reaching the top of the mountain, he sighed with tears of joy. He threw his arms out in great jubilation. In his zeal he knocked himself off balance and fell off the side of the mountain.   As he hurtled through space down the mountain side, his arm caught over a meager tree branch growing out the side of the rock, almost ripping his arm from its socket. There was not as much as a fingernail's hold anywhere and only sheer rocks straight above and below him. He desperately held onto the branch for his life.

After a few minutes in this position, his arm in great pain, Harry started to scream aloud for help. He heard a voice coming from above. "Harry, this is God." Harry says, "Great. God, I need help. Please help me." God said, "Okay, Harry, follow these instructions. Let go of the branch." Harry looked up, down and around and said,

"Is there anyone else up there?"

Letting go is one of the hardest things we do. We are conditioned to stay in control and to have all the answers. When going through really hard times, the dark night of the soul, our conditioning fails us completely. Depending on the depth and breadth of this void, we truly must use all our might to let go.

When we speak to God
we are said to be praying,
when God speaks to us
we are said to be schizophrenic!

Lily Tomlin

Sometimes we need more than what we, our friends and family can offer us. In these times of pain and confusion it is important to consider seeking professional guidance as a means to an end—to gain clarity and focus. Find someone who is there for you to help walk through the scattered puzzle pieces.

PROMISE:
This too shall pass. You're going to make it.

Chapter 15

STAGE 7: Surrender

*One thing that comes out of myths
is that at the bottom of the abyss
comes the voice of salvation.
The black moment is the moment when
the real message of transformation is going to come.
At the darkest moment comes the light.*

Joseph Campbell
The Hero's Journey

BEYOND THE FINITE

The Stage of Surrender (Figure 22) is a time when we begin to look beyond our finite minds and abilities. Thoughts about "how it should work" and "how things should be" are only met with more frustration and spent energy. We accept that where we've been is changing or is over and gone, that it's time to let go and move on. Letting go in this stage is the act of acceptance that there must be a greater picture that we cannot see. We trust that somehow the solution will work out. Our part in unveiling the solution is to get out of our own way.

Surrender, trust and hope can come easily—or not. It all depends on how invested, loyal and committed we are to any specific belief or belief system. It is said that "Pain is inevitable. Suffering is optional." Our struggle in and with life depends on how long we want to remain in struggle. As discussed earlier, the more conscious one becomes, the more flexible a person is to letting go and to experiencing the internal shift process. There can actually be a joy in finding out that you don't know something! That there are other ways of "seeing" things, other ways of believing and, ultimately, living.

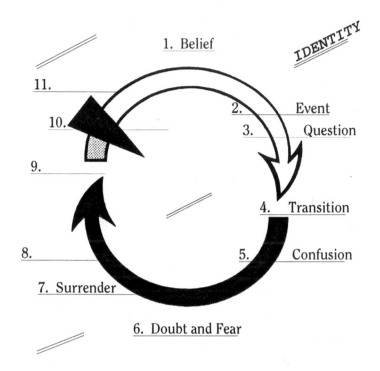

Figure 22 The ReDecisions 11-Stage Model - STAGE 7

Disillusionment with yourself must precede Enlightenment.

Vernon Howard
The Mystic Path to Cosmic Power

Surrendering and trusting in the transition process can feel like a total release and relief. It can feel like a healing when we finally let go of the struggle to know the answers and to the need for control. To let go to hope means to give up attachment and control, deep down trusting that all will be right again.

LETTING GO

Letting go means different things to different people. It can, for example, mean a huge blow to the ego when the shift is to grow out of conditioned beliefs about being perfect, being saintly or being in control and the best. Although it would seem like a good thing to let go and be more relaxed in life, for someone who has been hyper-vigilant about being good, right and (overly) responsible, this change feels threatening and like being *out* of control. These beliefs are hooked to and woven into the person's ego. Remember, the identity? Not being this way feels uncomfortable, out of balance and vulnerable.

Consider the crab who must push off its shell every time it outgrows it. It is naked and vulnerable in a sea of crab-eating creatures until it builds a new, bigger and better-fitting shell It's "new normal,"

TOUCHSTONE:
Pushing through fear is less frightening than living with the underlying fear that comes from a feeling of helplessness and powerlessness. It's easier than living with regrets. "I wish I had . . ."

One of the surrendering and acceptance point transitions shared by well-known corporate trainer, Tom Peters, is that he felt great to have turned 45. The reason? "When you look under the hood of a car, you don't have to act like you know what's under there anymore." Letting go of old egos, "false-self" masks, attitudes and energies is quite relieving. This can happen at any age, about anything.

Other examples of mental model shifts through surrender may include:

OLD: I have to be good and liked by everyone.
NEW: It's okay to be who I am and some people may not like me.

OLD: I have to do "it" alone.
NEW: No one does anything alone. It's okay to ask for and receive help.

OLD: I should know everything and never ask questions. People will think I'm stupid.
NEW: It's impossible to know everything. It's all right to ask questions.

OLD: I shouldn't ask for my needs to be met; others are more important.
NEW: I have needs like everyone else. It's okay to ask for what I want.

OLD: It's not okay to want money or material possessions. What I have is good enough.
NEW: Life is about enjoying all of its creations. I can enjoy financial freedom and the material goods I choose in my life.

OLD: It's not okay to be angry; I should always be happy.
NEW: Anger is normal and natural. I do feel angry at times, and it's okay to feel it, and express it, in healthy ways.

We are healed of our suffering only by experiencing it to the full.

Marcel Proust

Pain of the mind is worse than pain of the body.

Publilius Syrius

OLD: It's not okay to have opinions. Others might disagree with me.

NEW: Having opinions makes me a whole human being. It's okay if others don't agree, that's normal.

My favorite piece of music is the one we hear all the time if we are quiet.

John Cage
Classical music composer

And so on.

EXERCISE:

Take time to think about the mental models that are limiting and blocking you from truly enjoying life and from living with more calm and freedom.
❧ *Is it time to surrender?*
❧ *Is it time to be open to trust yourself and the process?*
❧ *What are you tired of holding on to?*

I often ask in my programs, and to about anyone I meet, *"Are you living your life's purpose? If not, why not? And what are you going to do about it?"* Life is very short. We begin dying the day we are born. There are no guarantees. So surrendering, trusting the process and opening our own door of hope for a brighter future are some of the ways we can enjoy the time we have. Feeling "naked" and not in control once in a while is very good for us.

EXERCISE:
One of the ways to find out what limits and blocks you have set up for yourself and, therefore, areas to surrender to, is through listening to your "statements of deprivation."

The following sentence completions will lead you to see areas of your life that keep you stuck. Some are future "to do's," others are regrets. Either way, they are limiting mindsets. These are opportunities for change, to let go and to move on— opportunities and challenges to create healthy and proactive mental models for a more open, flexible life.

Someday when . . ., then I'll . . . .
    "Someday when's" don't always come. What are you waiting for?

If I could only . . ., then . . . .
Why don't you do it?

My life will be better when . . . .
And maybe it won't. Do it or don't do it.

If only . . . .
Take charge or let go.

If . . . were different, then . . . .
It/they may not change. And even if it/they did, "then..." may not change anyway.

If only I would be . . . .
Then do it.

If only I would feel . . . .
Then change.

I wish that I had . . . .
The past is gone. Forgive it. Move on.

HOPE

Hope is a fertile emptiness—that time still in between the known and the unknown. Beneath the frozen ground of winter is a germinating, rooting of the next "known." There is a glimmer of light. Take a deep breath, "I'm going to make it."

THE LIFE LESSON:
Trust yourself.

When life keeps you in the dark baby, that's when you start looking at the stars.

Tess
Touched By An Angel
Television Show

Faith is an oasis in the heart which will never be reached by the caravan of thinking.

Kahlil Gibran
Sand and Foam

> *This life is a test—it is only a test.*
> *If it had been an* actual *life,*
> *you would have received further instructions*
> *on where to go and what to do.*
>
> Sign on the Post Office wall

Chapter 16

STAGE 8: Evaluation

We are not here just to survive and live long...
We are here to live and know life in its multi-dimensions,
to know life in its richness, in all its variety.
And when a man lives multi-dimensionally,
explores all possibilities available,
never shrinks back from any challenge,
goes, rushes to it, welcomes it, rises to the occasion,
then life becomes a flame, life blooms.

Bhagwan Shree Rajneesh

You've surrendered, let go. Now what? It is time to Evaluate (Figure 23) where you've been, where you're going and what the bigger picture looks like.

FAITH

It is through faith that we enter the Evaluation Stage as grief, anger and fear may continue. Just like seeing the trapeze bar coming to you in midair, you have faith that it's moving toward you and your grasp. Still not always seeing clearly the new direction, it is time to begin to take action toward the new, yet Unknown Territory.

The Evaluation Stage is another questioning period. "What if this new idea *is* true?" "What if this *is* the way it really is?" Like radar, the "What if's...?" will seek answers and some sort of completion, resolve or solution.

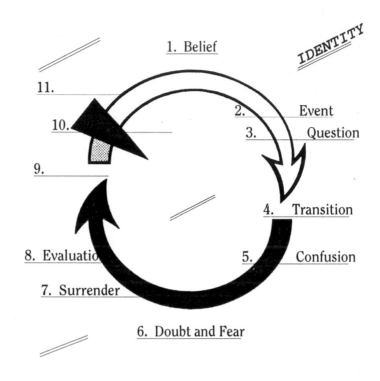

Figure 23 The ReDecisions 11-Stage Model - STAGE 8

FRIEND OR FOE:
GROWING STRONGER OR GROWING BEYOND

Asking input and feedback from others can be very helpful in Evaluating your choices. Whether it's through books, workshops, conversations with friends or professional guidance, it's important not to do it all alone. Remember, you will find those who understand your search and will want to help pull you up out of the crab bucket to freedom. Still others will be negative, even sabotaging, to keep you in the bucket with them.

So, part of the grief and loss of this growth and change process is that you may see it is time to leave some relationships behind. It's kind of like graduating from the High School of Life, ready to go on to the College of Life Classes. You may find family, friends and acquaintances who ask, beg, plead, demand and shame you to get back into third grade with them. They'll want you to scrunch yourself into that little desk and sit through those lessons one more time, because by golly, "It's good enough for you."

Suffering threatens to make life
meaningless.
That is its greatest danger.
It is up to each of us
to restore meaning.

Deepak Chopra
The Deeper Wound

When participants in my programs agonize over family and other relationship frustrations, I ask "If your family wasn't your family, would they be your friends?" The answer, "no." Some, many, of them would not. This is not a judgment—remember, they are not bad people, they are just living out of their conditioned beliefs and mental models.

So if we wouldn't want to know some of our family members if they weren't our family, then why do we lose ourselves in *their* life dramas? Why do we give up and over our power and life energy to their "crab bucket" mentalities and limitations? That *is* our problem. That *is* our responsibility.

TOUCHSTONE:
There is no one "out there."
There is no "they."

SOCIAL SUPPORT SYSTEM

Your social support systems, made up of whomever you choose, are many things to you throughout a lifetime:

- ✎ They are enduring, interpersonal ties to groups of people who can be relied upon to provide emotional support, assistance and resources in times of need.

- ✎ They are people who provide feedback and who share similar standards and values.

- ✎ They are those who support you through times of crisis and calm and with whom feelings can be shared without fear of condemnation.

- ✎ They help maintain your psychological, spiritual and physical well-being over time.

- ✎ They share information leading you to believe that you are cared for and loved, esteemed and valued, and that you belong to a network of communication and mutual obligation.

It is important to know who your "real" friends are when going through change of any kind, especially long and hard times of transition. Some will be weeded out because they won't be there for you; others will be too needy when you are the one who needs nurturing and attention at the moment.

Go behind the apparent circumstances of the situation and locate the love in yourself and in all others involved in the situation.

Mother Teresa

EXERCISE:
Using the following headings, list those individuals you feel support you in these areas of your life:
- Home
- Work
- Social/Sexual
- Emotional/Feelings
- Spiritual
- Fears
- Goals/Dreams
- Play

Examine your list. It is important that you don't have only one person's name under each of these.

I couldna done it without my players.

Casey Stengel
New York Yankes Manager
On winning the 1958 World Series

Make many friends in the world. To set yourself up to be dependent solely on one other, or a small handful of people, will create a second crisis when they are unable to be there for you. No matter what their reasons, you will have no one.

Now, think through this list of headings again with your circle of friends and family in mind. Are you the only one on any of their lists? It is just as important to prevent this from happening. If you feel someone is too dependent on you, your energy and time, help them to understand that they need to have more friends and support as well. You don't want to set yourself up to be in this position of "rescuer" either. It is not fair to you or them.

TOUCHSTONE:
Rescuers become the persecuted.

LETTING GO: BLAME AND FORGIVENESS

Part of our letting go of outdated identity and limited belief is to let go of blaming others for holding us back. Whether they abused us, confused us or just generally refused us as children, and even as adults, we can choose to let go of the loss and pain and move on.

Basically, if you're alive, your parents/family did their job. Now, it's your job. It's your life. Move it. Life's short!

Is that not enough for you? Should they have done it differently? More, better or whatever? Sorry. It's over. They did the best they could with the information they had and with the mental programming and conditioning they grew up with.

TOUCHSTONE:
The tragedy of life is not in dying, but in *not living*.

EXERCISE:
Make a list of the blaming and negative thoughts, statements and comments you hear yourself make about others. They may be statements that you say out loud or just in your mind, but they are there.

Blame keeps us stuck. Review these issues of hurt, pain, loss and distrust. Move them into a place of transition. Here is a simple, to-the-point definition of forgiveness: Forgiveness is not forgiving another for what they've done wrong or against you; forgiveness is forgiving another for not being or doing what you *expected*. Confront these issues to deal with them or to let them go. Either way, move them out to open up the door to your own freedom. Detach.

A note on forgiving and forgetting abusive situations. Letting go of painful experiences is important to our ability to move on in our lives. We need not forget the situation, though, in that we need to have grown from it to develop healthy, strong boundaries against being hurt or abused again. Life flows when we know who we are, where we start and where others end.

The grudge you hold onto
is like a hot coal
that you intend to throw
at somebody else, but
you're the one who gets burned.

Buddha

TOUCHSTONE:
The pain of dying comes from unfinished business.

DESERVING

Feeling unworthy and undeserving are often conditioned mindsets that keep us struggling, angry, fearful, blaming and stuck. How much "good stuff" in life do you think you deserve? Do you have to wait longer, or work harder, or be smarter in order to be "good enough?" Do you feel unworthy of happiness and the good life has to offer? If you're not sure, the following exercise may help you.

EXERCISE:
Go down the following list of Deserving statements. Mark, mentally or with a pencil, the ones you feel uncomfortable about. Which ones do you feel you don't *deserve?*

I DESERVE...

to be loved.
to make my own life choices.
to be successful.
to get my needs met.
to set my own goals.
to feel good about myself.
to be given to without conditions.
to be talked to gently.
to be seen as capable.
to be taken care of.
to be seen as lovable.
to feel a part of (fill in).
to have financial freedom.
to be touched with love and kindness.
to be treated with care and kindness.
to live a fulfilling life.
to enjoy my sexuality.
to be in healthy relationships.
to laugh and have fun.
to know more than others.
to take care of myself.
to have time for myself.
to be calm.
to be excited.
to just "be."

to be respected.
to be treated nicely.
to be liked.
to be listened to.
to be understood.
to enjoy life.
to be rewarded.
to be supported.
to be healthy.
to live my dreams.
to be honored.
to be talented.
to relax.
to be happy.
to ask for help.
to be acknowledged.
to be smart.
to win.
to be selfish.
to achieve.
to be complimented.
to be wealthy.
to have the best.
to receive.

Did you mark any?
1. If you did, what is your belief about yourself regarding the specific deserving statement?
2. Where did you learn this about yourself?
3. What if...you let go of it?
4. What if...you claim your right to its truth for you and live with this new belief, new identity?
5. How would/will you be different if you believe it's true?
6. What will change in you, and in your life, if you live from this new belief?

If you feel uncomfortable with this opportunity for a new identity created by a new belief system, that's all right. Remember, mental models can die slow and hard, and our loyalties to them can be amazingly strong, even when they are clearly unhealthy for us.

EXERCISE:
Try on some new identities and see how they feel. Choose one of the statements you marked on the I Deserve list. Take a few minutes and create a new movie in your mind. Imagine yourself believing, living and acting out this new belief about yourself. How does it look? How does it feel? What has changed? How do others treat you with your new identity?

Now, try on another new identity. Make another new mental movie. Be aware of your feelings about it. Can you make the leap?

TOUCHSTONE:
We teach people how to treat us.

RESPECT

If you continue attracting people who treat you in ways that you don't like, you might check out how you are teaching them that it's okay to do so. The more undeserving and unworthy you believe you are, the more you will tend to attract people who feed on this victim-martyr role. Again, these people are not bad. Like you, they have areas of their lives where they don't honor themselves. They are still living out limiting beliefs that don't serve them or others. Where they feel they don't deserve, they unfortunately then project and dump on you.

TOUCHSTONE:
The universe abhors a vacuum.

If you create a new identity to be filled with new beliefs and reflections of people, places and things to match it, it will be filled. If you go back to your old belief, only the old "fillings" can remain. Some choice, huh?

It's like going down to the beach and digging a hole in the sand. If you don't fill it up with a beach ball or a bucket or something, it will soon

I am always with myself, and it is I who am my tormentor.

Leo Tolstoy

fill in with sand again. You have to take *action* to change the contents of the "filling."

Remember the Reactionary Default Response Menu? If you don't put in new beliefs and ways of thinking and behaving, your mental computer will Default back to the old programmed responses. That's nature.

The flight attendant on an airplane will instruct passengers that in the event of an emergency the oxygen mask will fall from the ceiling panel. When this happens PUT YOUR MASK ON FIRST, "THEN" HELP THE PERSON NEXT TO YOU." Why? Because if you're dead you can't help anyone!

TOUCHSTONE:
Create healthy boundaries in which you take care of yourself "first".

Teach people the way you want to be treated by *respecting yourself first*. They will follow suit. If they don't follow suit, they will move on—and in some cases they will be cleaned out of your life completely. This vacuum creates room for the new, respectful people whom you attract. Why not go for the positive, healthy, fun ones? *You deserve it.*

GOOD ENOUGH

Deserving issues, in the Evaluation Stage, mirror statements of feeling or not feeling "good enough."

EXERCISE:
1. List any areas in your life where you do not feel or think that you are good enough.
2. How does this look in your life? How does it show up or manifest itself?
3. Where did you learn that you were not good enough?
4. What act, accomplishment, object or title would make you feel good enough?

Number 4 asks you to be responsible for your own self-esteem. It's up to you to create actions or events that will support you in feeling good and okay about yourself and that make you feel like you *fit in*. The *in* will be whatever you choose it to be.

The mass of men lead lives of quiet desperation and go to the grave with the song still in them.

Henry David Thoreau
American Writer

It's likely that you've had others condition you to not love or trust yourself throughout your life. Remember the shadow? It was surely a reflection of their own insecurities. Whatever they couldn't deal with—their shadow side—they projected onto you. You became their dumping ground. Sorry.

And, no one has ever done anything *to* you. They did, and do, something *for* themselves, due to their own conditioned beliefs, and you happen to have been in their lives at the time. If it wasn't you, it quite likely would have been someone else.

As an adult, it is your job to clean up the dump and clear out the garbage. No one can do this work for you. Sorry again. It's up to you to evaluate your life options and choices and find ways to teach yourself how to feel "good enough." To love yourself through your changes.

I'm good enough;
I'm smart enough;
and, doggoneit,
people like me.

Stuart Smalley
Saturday Night Live

EXERCISE:
This exercise on "feeling good enough" is always interesting. Think about something you've done or that has happened in your life that made you feel rich or successful, like you "made it." Now, in order to have more control over these experiences, go through the list below, proactively deciding actions to take to nurture and support yourself.

What act, accomplishment, object or title would make you...
• feel powerful?
• feel confident?
• have a higher self-image or self-concept?
• feel rich?
• feel successful?
• feel complete?
• feel okay about yourself?
• feel like you've *made it*?
• feel fulfilled?
• feel loved?
• feel worthy?
• feel deserving?
• feel calm?
• feel good enough?
• feel like you belong?

Let me share one of the many actions I have taken to shift my mental model and identity regarding feeling rich, successful, confident, powerful and complete. For many years I have "seen" in my mental movie about my successful life a stone-wood home with Indian rugs hanging over the rafters and staircase banisters. This entire vision is part of my mindset that says, "Someday when I have this, I will have made it. I will have connected with my life vision and purpose."

After I first moved to Denver in 1986, I had little money due to my college loan payments, low paying health care jobs and life. One of my first speaking jobs (new identity) was in Vail. On the way back to Denver, I stopped in Georgetown to visit the shops. In the last shop I entered I noticed a stack of Indian rugs on the floor. They were all different and each beautiful.

I had very little money in the bank and wasn't buying non-essential items. But I had about $80.00 cash in my pocket from selling my lecture cassette tapes at the program earlier that day. The rug that "called to me" was $65.00. After a little agonizing, I bought it.

When I returned home to my small one bedroom apartment, in lieu of rafters or banisters, I folded the rug over the arm of my couch. The purchase of that rug (65 big dollars!) was one of many turning points for me in my change of identity about deserving issues. My pattern was to see my life "all together" when I had the whole enchilada. The rug alone was what I needed right then. The rug was a gift to myself, *toward* my future dream, that helped me to *feel* rich, worthy, deserving and successful.

TOUCHSTONE:
There are no "Someday whens. . .."

That little rug is still on my couch today, along with many more I've added to my home over the years.

GIFTS OF GROWTH

What simple acts of kindness can you offer yourself to help you feel needed, wanted and other positive, nurturing emotions? If you don't learn to give yourself *gifts of growth*, you may wait and wish for others to do it. They may and they may not.

Here is another quick example of how a simple event helped to shift my identity. I received a phone call from my friend, Michael, letting me know he would be arriving at the airport 20 minutes earlier than planned and asking me to meet him there. I knew he was flying in from Seattle, and...it takes longer than 20 minutes to fly to Denver. When I asked where he was calling from, he said, "the airplane."

Life is like a game of cards. The hand that is dealt you represents determinism; the way you play it is free will.

Jawaharlal Nehru

Now, for about $8.00 (fees may vary!) and a credit card, you, too, can call from an airplane! But for me, at that time in my life, that phone call was one of those "Aha's." Okay, maybe more like a "Wow!" I just felt so rich and important. Somebody *I know* is calling *me* from an airplane! Today it would be normal. Then, it was not a common occurrence in my life and was truly amazing to me.

Whatever the answers may be to the questions in the "feeling good enough" exercise, start to create them. It can make major shifts in your view and perception of the world, of others and, more importantly, of yourself.

DEPRIVATION

When we fail to do nurturing, loving things for ourselves, we can feel deprived and angry, which leads to envy, resentment and jealousy of others in the world. Have you ever heard yourself or others say, "Must be nice...." (to have, be, do or whatever they are jealous about)? Well, just to help you out on this one, the answer to "Must be nice...." is, "It is!" You might want to remember that!

Another statement of deprivation is, "Oh, it's good enough," but then to complain later that, in fact, it's not. Change your deserving mental model about yourself. Your "feel goods" could be as simple as my rug was for me.

TOUCHSTONE:
There are no "points in Heaven."

By the way, there are no *points in heaven*. I know many, many people who are trying to be good and do everything right *down here* so that someday they'll get points "up there." Well, sorry again. Living your life fully each day is the reward for living your life. And, *if* I'm wrong, *trying to be good* is very different than living a complete and honest life where you will mess up, a lot, and *still* be good. When I finally figured this mental model out, I also had to let go of "Life is fair and people are honest." It isn't and they aren't. That's life.

WHAT IF?

Throughout the Evaluation Stage you will be asking yourself to look at new pictures of yourself, to rearrange the puzzle pieces to see how they can fit in another way. "What if this new idea *is* true?" "What if this *is* the way it really is?" The "What if's...?" will seek answers and ways to create and support the new direction. You will undoubtedly have to add some new puzzle pieces and throw some out in the

*Holding on
only hurts the one
who's holding on.
Letting go
heals the heart of the same.
Looking back,
and wishing it were different,
only holds on to the pain.*

"Holding On,"
lyrics by Kim Wolinski
In Thanks & Gratitude album

process.

The more "What if's?" you ask yourself and others, and listen for answers, the easier the process will be. The answers—asking you to grow, change and connect to yourself at a deeper level—may sometimes scare you. They certainly will surprise you.

NEW NORMALS

The way your life has been to date has been "normal." In the process of evaluation you are creating the new puzzle, the "new normal" for your life. The example earlier of my friend calling me from an airplane is now a "new normal" for me.

EXERCISE:
Practice some new normals. Think of a couple of things you have been wishing for, dreaming about, setting goals for. Then, where possible, go try them out. That's right. As an example, you have been wanting a new or different car. You even know exactly which one you want. Go to the dealership and sit in it. Ask questions. Drive it— practice your "new normal."

Deprivation and "someday whens" keep us from NOW. I practice new normals with house shopping. I go to the neighborhoods I think I'd like to live in and I tour all the "Open Houses." It doesn't cost anything but my time. They're open and available for me to check out. You may be surprised to find that you *don't* want something after trying it out. So, clean it out and move on to the next vision.

When we can "see" our new path leading to the new idea, thought or belief, we are well on our way into Stage 9, Passage.

You can feel for people and adore people and still *want to have a nice sweater.*

Joan Rivers

VI

─•◦●◦•─

Beginnings

─•◦●◦•─

*The purpose of life
is to be that self which one truly is.*

Soren Kierkegaard

The real alienation in our time is not from society, but from self.

Marilyn Ferguson
The Aquarian Conspiracy

Chapter 17

STAGE 9: Passage

*Fear is often an indication
I am avoiding myself.*

Hugh Prather

You've now gone through the Stages of identifying some belief that has developed the identity that you live. An event happens that requires you to question your belief and your identity. This creates a movement, a transition into confusion, doubt and fear, grief and loss, an emptying out into the void, in the process of change. Finding the strength to let go, through surrender and trust, gives hope to the feeling that you're "going to make it."

Now comes time for evaluation of the puzzle pieces. You ask more questions to guide you to resolution of whether to hold onto the old mental model or to move on and choose a new one. Here, then, is the age-old abyss, which knights in shining armor, mystics, heroes and heroines of all times must ponder—Stage 9, The Passage (Figure 24).

TOUCHSTONE:
Fear of success is greater than fear of failure.

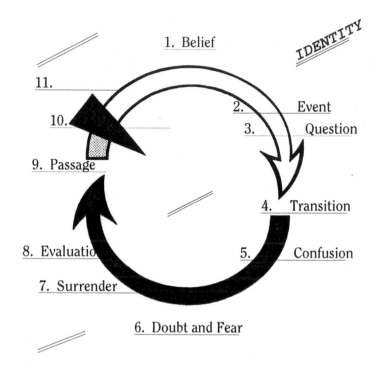

Figure 24 The ReDecisions 11-Stage Model - STAGE 9

FORKED ROAD

The Passage Stage can be the wings that carry us into the light of newness, or it can be our abyss, where we hesitate too long and fall back into the darkness. There are several forks in the road at this Stage. We take the information from the preceding Stages and through the evaluation process and then choose one of the following three paths.

FORK 1: Mental Model Shift.
> You get the "Oh!", creating a mental model shift to move on to ReDecide, a new belief and new identity.

FORK 2: ReCommit.
> You get the "Oh!", creating a mental model shift that recognizes, in fact, that your old belief *was* right. You choose from an "Action-ary," conscious Menu and ReCommit to your belief.

FORK 3: Black Hole.

You decide that your intuition, inner guidance and everyone else's support and help is wrong. Change is too uncomfortable and you are not going to change even though it will be worse than before and is not healthy. You stop and ReTurn.

The Passage Stage is like a teeter-totter. FORKS 1 and 2 are examples of doing all the work, making it through the dragon-infested swamps—the Stages of Questions, Confusion, Doubt and Fear, and Evaluation. This takes us to the middle of the teeter-totter (Figure 25).

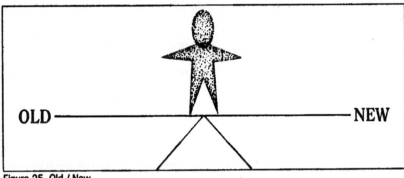

Figure 25 Old / New

Anything you are attached to,
let it go.
Go to places that scare you.

Pema Chödrön
The Places That Scare You

We get that *one more puzzle piece* of information, 51 percent, or whatever it takes to create that internal "shift," and the teeter then totters into the new land of beliefs (Figure 26).

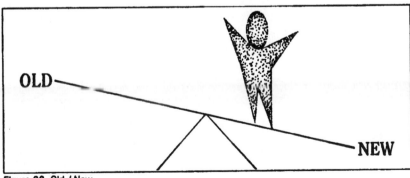

Figure 26 Old / New

RECOMMITMENT AND TRANSFORMATION

I've already given several examples of FORK 1: Mental Model Shift, "getting it" and shifting into the new belief, the new mental model, and I will talk more about it in the next chapter. Here is a good example of FORK 2: ReCommitment.

FORK 2.
You get the "Oh!", creating a mental model shift that recognizes, in fact, that your old belief *was* right. You choose from an "Action-ary," conscious Menu and ReCommit to your belief.

I recently was reacquainted with a fellow I knew in high school, 24 years ago. For 21 years, Doug had been driving a semi-trailer truck. He quit three months before he turned 40, mid-life transition time. He also moved, changed some relationships and quit smoking three weeks before his birthday. He was feeling good about most of the changes he had created, yet he was unfocused and unclear about just what he wanted to be doing and where he belonged.

Doug and I first talked after his birthday. After a couple of conversations, he surprised himself with *redeciding to go back* to driving. He was back on the road within three weeks. Outside of the "I told you so's" from old trucker friends and family, he's glad to be back in his element, where he says "he belongs," to what he truly loves doing.

Unless you try to do something beyond what you have already mastered, you will never grow.

Ronald E. Osborn

There are many times that our journey *under* can *bring us back to where we started*. Of course, you can never really return to the exact place where you started. You are different and your outlook will have changed due to new input—you *undergo* some sort of transformation. When this redecisions cycle leads to recommitment, the transformation usually includes an increase in self-esteem, self-confidence and a deeper trust in yourself—creating a new identity of self-trust.

In Doug's case, he needed to stop and rest for a while. He needed a reset —to take some time out with family and friends, to reassess and redecide his life choices with all the puzzle pieces in front of him. His redecision brought him back to himself on a higher level on the Spiral of Life.

EXERCISE:
What redecisions have you made that have led you to recommit to yourself? How did this experience make you feel?

THE BLACK HOLE

Of course, there is always the option to do nothing. FORK 3 is an example of having the input to change, getting all the way to the middle of the teeter totter and deciding, for whatever reason, that we're not going to make the leap (Figure 27).

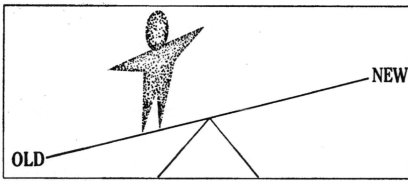

Figure 27 Old / New

There is a paradox at the juncture of the Passage Stage. You let go and move on, or you hold on and get stuck. You detach or attach. Because this process is so important, the abyss deserves undivided attention. In Chapter 20, The Black Hole, I will expand on this interesting act of free will.

EXERCISE:
Think of a time that you went through Stages 1-8 and came to the passage.

1. Did you take FORK 1 or 2 or 3?
2. How has it affected your life?

   If it didn't shift, and positive growth was not created, what can/will you do today to move beyond the passage? Is it time to move beyond your fears and limits?

By your stumbling,
the world is perfected.

Sri Aurobindo

*Life literally abounds in comedy
if you just look around you.*

Mel Brooks
Filmmaker, Actor

Chapter 18

STAGE 10: Mental Model Shift

❦

Shift Happens.

❦

Remember my definition of a mental model shift from Chapter 2? After moving through Stages 1-9, the information (puzzle pieces) weaves in and out of your mind and body, triggering little switches and gears along the way, moving you into the next level of understanding regarding this belief or belief system (Figure 28).

THE SHIFT

There is a literal *shift* when we "get it." It takes place inside us, and suddenly we really *know* the answer. Like learning how to ride a bike, to run a new computer program or to conquer a new dance step, once that shift has occurred, we will always know how to do it. Every cell in your body "gets it." "Oh!" "Aha!" "Now I get it." And you will never be the same again. Perhaps you just needed to know that you could do something, giving you a needed shot of self-confidence shift.

TOUCHSTONE:
There's no going back to Kansas, once you've been to OZ.
THE GOOD NEWS is, you can't go back after you know too much.
THE BAD NEWS is, you can't go back after you know too much.

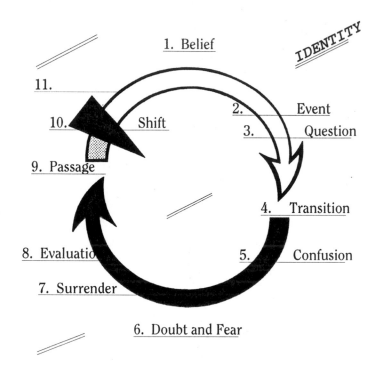

Figure 28 The ReDecisions 11-Stage Model - STAGE 10

CELLULAR KNOWING

As with most of our evolving and unfolding life process, the shift may be sudden or it may be gradual. Either way, a mental model shift occurs when we *internalize the knowledge*. It becomes part of the fabric of who we are, that "knowing" sense. It's a "cellular shift" of knowing that you know. We are never again the same.

At this point, it becomes more than an intellectual understanding. When the shift does come, there is no struggle. It is integrated into one's mindset as "of course this is the way to do it!" "Why didn't I get this before?" "How could I have not seen this?"

THE CANNING JARS

After moving into my new apartment several years ago, my friend Cathy stayed and offered to help unpack my kitchen boxes and put everything away before she left. We each grabbed a box and started in. Cathy unwrapped newspaper from jars (quart and pint jars from pickles, salad dressing and the like) and put the jars into the kitchen cupboard. After about eight empty jars, she asked me if the whole box was filled with empty jars. I said that it was. When she asked me why,

I just stared at her for a couple of seconds (the mind shift synapses were gearing up). I replied, "They're for canning." She asked me, "Do you can?" I said, "No." "Then why are you keeping these?" she asked. I answered, "Well...*because that's what they're for*. And I don't want to throw out *perfectly good glass jars*."

Well, we laughed long and hard about this one, while putting them all back into the box. What is this belief and where did it come from?

The Belief/Value
You can foods because it is cheaper, and then you store them for long-term use. You recycle and use everything to the "nth" degree, including rinsing out bread bags and hanging them on the clothes line to reuse again! You don't waste anything worth using, because as we *all* know, a) it's wasteful to throw things out that are still good, and b) "You never know when you're going to need it."

Where did I learn this mental model?
I grew up in a farming community in the Midwest. My family grew, canned, cooked, pickled, stored, froze, potted, made and stewed almost everything. There weren't options for some of these things. It was a lifestyle to recycle, reuse, wear hand-me-downs and the like. Some of these cultural patterns remain, and still are, pretty much the norm.

Is this good or bad?
For me, they are very good. No, I redecided that I don't need to collect multiple empty containers in my cupboards. I can recycle them in new ways due to the evolution of recycling programs. (Thank goodness!)

I value the activity of recycling, reusing and caring for the planet. It is a stable part of my belief system and it has served me very well. I'll keep it!

HABIT, TRANCE AND UNCONSCIOUS PATTERNS
The bottom line is, I didn't even know that I was doing it. It was a normal, natural activity and a conditioned, learned action. Like the shadow illustrations in Chapter 6, the overall mental program is about a lifestyle and livelihood that was my childhood and my family's way of life. Why would I have questioned it, until someone else did?

Some mental models change without our realization, some require conscious work and effort, and others, like my canning story, surprise us! From individuals to corporations to government and world politics, it works the same. We get locked into mental models that are ineffective and costly. To many, it seems easier to stay blocked in the old, known, comfortable categories and boxes. Just doing it the way they've always done it is good enough. Because, remember, boxes equal security and Known Territory, they feel "safe" like the known land on the Dragon Map.

CREAM CHEESE AND THE BLENDER

As a child, I would go on family vacations across country to visit our good friends, Annette and Kenny. On one of our visits Annette was making some snacks. As I sat on the kitchen counter I watched as she dropped a package of cream cheese into the blender to get it smooth, adding spices for a chip dip. (Now, if you've ever done this, you know it takes a while to get all the cream cheese back off the insides of the container, especially when it has those scalloped sides.) After Annette had spun it around for a while, she clicked the wooden spoon around a couple of times, getting about 80 percent of the cream cheese out, and then put the container in the dishwater to wash later. I about fell off the counter! She didn't use a spatula (or her finger) to get the other 20 percent out of that glass pitcher. As my eyes grew wide staring at that pitcher in the dish water with cream cheese glaring up at me, I heard the synapses shooting off in my head. Creating still another mental model and assumption, "Wow, they must be rich."

The Belief/Value (My "truth")
You don't waste anything, especially food.

Where did I learn this mental model?
From my family and culture growing up.

Is this good or bad?
Very good. Works for me!
I'll keep this one.

ReDecision
I'll keep this one.

Oh, and another shift. I have since learned that leaving 20 percent of the cream cheese in the blender does not mean that people are rich.

TOUCHSTONE:
Choose to be more and more conscious of unconscious conditioning.

In order to transform your old/present identity into your new/future identity and self-image, you must become conscious of unconscious conditioning. One of the best ways to do this is with good friends who

Look about you.
The environment is burning up
in a hundred, a thousand places,
worldwide.
But there is no fire escape here,
no "out," no other solution
than a shift
in knowing who we are.

Jim Nollman

know that they can hold a mirror up to you, to help open your mind and eyes to discrepancies and beliefs that may be harming you or keeping you stuck.

These examples are mild and certainly not earth shaking in the whole of life. Unfortunately, there are severe unconscious beliefs and values that people live out that can truly hurt themselves and others. These include bigotry, racism, sexism, criticism, abuse and others that are violent and harmful to everyone.

EXERCISE:
#1:
Go through your house "like a stranger." Act like you've never been there before and, in fact, don't know the person who lives there. Question this person's taste in design, decor, storage, food buys, knickknacks (tchotkes—all those little frou-frou items you have to dust around), clothing and so on. See if you can get outside yourself far enough to discern what might be changed to help you feel freer, less locked into "have to's and must's", or otherwise more positive.

#2:
Ask a friend or two to stroll through your house and ask questions about why you have or do some things. It doesn't mean you have to change anything, and you may discover unconscious conditioning for your review.

#3:
Ask your close friends, who you can trust to support you, to be a mirror for you. Invite them to give you feedback on yourself, your lifestyle, your relationships and communication skills, your physical appearance and your personality traits.

Remember: when asking for feedback, it is your job to "take it like a willow tree." Take a deep breath, be open and flexible to their input and feedback, and laugh a lot. Take what makes sense to you and leave the rest. Some things you might change, others you may find are perfect for who you are and how you want to be right now. The point is, *be willing and open to find out. Be willing and open to change.*

MENTAL MODEL, MINDSET AND MINDSHIFT
Have you ever noticed that you tend to see what you believe you're going to see? You bring to a situation what you expect you're going to experience. In fact, you will subconsciously seek to prove through your experience that you were right.

TOUCHSTONE:
Your mind lives to be right.

We've heard children, and ourselves, comment after an experience they had already predicted they wouldn't enjoy, "See, I knew I wasn't going to like it." Unless you choose to be open to a mindshift—shifting your state of mind—you will continually get the same experience and cognitive feedback (although others around you may disagree with you). You might want to rent the movie *Groundhog Day* to advance this concept!

EXERCISE:
Is your mindset open to change?
If so, where might it be open to a mindshift?

Think about each of these relationships or issues in your life, and see if it's time to shift the way you think about them or it.

Mother	Neighbors	Your routines
Father	Co-workers	Your habits
Brother	Boss	Your body
Sister	Job	Eating habits
Spouse	Politics	Exercise habits
Children	Government	Your lifestyle
Friends	Religion	God
Other relationships	Money management	Life
Communication skills		Death
Add your own....		

1. Could you choose a more flexible mindset?
2. Could you be more open to other's beliefs?
3. Is it time to choose a different relationship with any one of these?
4. If so, what will the new relationship be? What will it look like?
5. What are you willing to *let go* of to make the change happen?

Asking effective questions invites shifts on an ongoing basis. Sometimes we don't even notice they are happening. We often just think, "Oh!"

If you fix on yourself
and your tradition,
believing you alone
have got "It,"
you've removed yourself from
the rest of mankind.

Joseph Campbell

GETTING TO "OH!"—MENTAL MODEL PARALYSIS

Some people avoid getting to "Oh!" like the plague. By refusing to be flexible and consider the possibility of change, you are choosing to remain in a limited mindset. It becomes a mental model block or a paralysis. This paralysis snuffs out creativity, vision, imagination and, ultimately, freedom and love.

Paralysis is created from conditioned fear, blame and resentment. These limitations create more limitations and fear. Over time, limitations and fear are acted out in anger, abuse, violence, depression and illness. The core belief is black or white, all or none rigid thinking: "I'm right, you're wrong." The fear is, "If I let go of my belief, I won't know who I am. I'll feel out of control and confused, and I don't like these feelings." People who feel this way have no new identity picture to think about or to "see" in their mind's eye. They have no goal toward which to move.

Anything dead coming back hurts.

Toni Morrison
from *Beloved*

TOUCHSTONE:
If you think in the same box long enough, it will become a coffin.

I've known people who would not change their mindsets because of the fear of others saying, "I told you so." Who is the loser here? They are. It doesn't matter what others think of your choices or that you have to take the long way around to figure something out. It matters only that you make the healthiest, proactive choices you can at the time. You'll never please everyone, and in trying to, you lose yourself. You have to live with the results.

LET GO— *SHIFT*
The alternative to mental model paralysis is to acknowledge the life/death/life cycle, endings, beginnings, and endings; to live a life of conscious openness to options. This mindset that life is always in motion, that there's an ebb and flow of change, creates awareness and choices to even more options and choices. Life is easier, more centered and grounded, flowing and flexible. Embracing death as part of life, then, is not so devastating.

Living life with an open mindset means that, while you live with and live out your life's beliefs system, you stay flexible to new ways of seeing, doing, being and knowing. Think of it as the pruning process. There are many trees that must be pruned every year in order to remain vital and resilient. We need pruning as well.

TIME AND REGRETS:
LETTING GO OF THE PAST
When you push against the changes that you and possibly others are

asking you to make, or against new choices others are encouraging of you, you waste time. You waste life itself. Wasting time creates regrets and self-blame. "I wish I would have...." "Why didn't I...." "If only I'd...."

TOUCHSTONE:
You can't get time back.

Worry, stress, fretfulness, rumination, anger, guilt, blame or fear only take up energy and time that could be used toward living life fully. These limiting uses of our effort and brain power keep us from using our potential, creativity and positive forward-focused energy for growth. These limits keep us from sharing life-fulfilling opportunities with others as well.

TOUCHSTONE:
From moment to moment we have the opportunity to choose how to use our life energy: to move toward or away from our own lives.

EXERCISE:
In your mind's eye, imagine yourself to be 95 years old. (If you are 95, give yourself another 10 or 20 years!) Now, at 95, look back over your life as it is today *and answer the following questions:*
1. How important were some of those decisions that I made?
2. Did I get caught up in other people's judgment and criticism of me? Why?
3. How was it that I gave in to other's needs and fears?
4. If I had to do my life over, I would have . . .
5. What kept me from taking risks?
6. What kept me from changing?
7. What I really want is . . .

With your list of things that you would do over, come back to yourself at this moment, and do the following:

1. Take action on the answers you listed. Move forward into your life, where possible.

Just Do It!

Nike Ad

2. Let go of regrets, guilt, shame and other "What's wrong with me? I'm so awful, stupid, slow..." thoughts. Ask yourself:

Question: Can I change it?
Answer: No.
Action: Then let it go.

Question: Can I change it?
Answer: Yes.
Action: Then do it.

The bottom line is, either do it or don't do it, but don't get caught in the middle feeling guilty and wrong.

Why do this exercise? As I discussed earlier, we need to stop once in a while and reset, "get out of ourselves" to be more objective with our lives. With all of our daily dramas, we tend to lose objectivity, clarity and focus. We need to "witness" our lives from the outside periodically. Get up in the "helicopter of life" and look down over the puzzle pieces. See how they are or are not fitting and take action to rearrange them for a better fit.

RITUALS:
ACKNOWLEDGE AND CELEBRATE YOUR POSITIVE CHANGE

Progress, growth, change—SHIFT! You need to acknowledge your growth and reward yourself for your hard work of letting go, for simply surviving some of life's hard times.

Whether you call it a ritual or possibly a rite of passage, it is important to make time for special celebrations and acknowledgments of your transformation.

TOUCHSTONE:
Celebrate yourself!

When I turned 30, as my transition into my third decade and other meanings of adulthood, I gave myself a rite of passage ritual celebration. I called it an *Unwedding Shower*! Two reasons: one, aging has always been a good thing for me, and I didn't mind celebrating it; second, well, I figured, "What if...I never get married? When do I get all the *stuff*?" So I made up and sent out 200 invitations to everyone I liked in my life, whether they knew me or not. The

As human beings we are made to surpass ourselves and are truly ourselves only when transcending ourselves.

Huston Smith

invitation gave the option to come without a gift, with a gift or even to add to my *registry*. Yes, that's right, I had a registry. I lived in Omaha at the time, and the store of choice was Canfields outdoor sports and equipment store. I explained in my invitation that if I never got married, I would never divide up, throw out, burn, abuse or give away any of the registry goods in a divorce. And if I ever did end up in a committed relationship, I would be able to share these wonderful gifts. It seemed like a win-win proposition to me.

How did it turn out? I received everything on my registry list and cash to buy extras. About 40 family and friends came to my celebration. I even received letters from two invited guests, Kenny Rogers and Shirley MacLaine. Kenny and Shirley each said they were glad to have been invited, but couldn't make it due to their tour schedules. I understood.

LIFE AS CHAPTERS, CYCLES, BEGINNINGS AND ENDINGS

Here are the stages of the redecisions transition process when consciously acknowledged: 1) Ending 2) Transition 3) Beginning 4) Acknowledgment 5) Celebration 6) Completion.

When I planned my celebration, I didn't know anything about ritual and rites of passage at the time. My guts just said, "Do this." What I didn't know, and couldn't have, was that just two months after my Unwedding Shower, I "got" the bigger picture of this rite of passage and knew that it was about *completion* for me. I had finished my graduate work the year before and felt very complete with that part of my life. Colorado called. I packed my car and moved (end of Student Life Chapter) on to the present and continuing, unfolding next Chapter of My Life (Entrepreneur Life Chapter). I am completing this Life Chapter as I write and beginning another.

EXERCISE:
Think about your life and its endings and beginnings, starting points and completions, the rituals and rites of passage that you have experienced. Create rituals for life transitions and special occasions.

Ritual, and the need to complete or start something, can be a conscious or a very unconscious experience. Like my Unwedding Shower, there are times when we find ourselves needing to stop, to get away, to throw out, to clean out or to renew some area of our lives. We don't always understand why; it's an inner pull that moves us

Every man who rises above the common level has received two educations: the first from his teachers; the second, more personal and important, from himself.

Edward Gibbon

through it. It is our own inner, personal cycles of nature. When you find yourself being "asked" from the inside out to regroup and rearrange, it is probably time to reevaluate your life's direction and choices and to redecide something. Enjoy it! Embrace it! Welcome it! Have fun.

LIFE LINES, EBB AND FLOW AND INITIATIONS

EXERCISE:
On the longest length of a piece of paper, draw a horizontal line. This is your LIFE LINE. At the left end of the line, mark a "0" and the year of your birth. At the right end of the line, mark your current age and year. Separate the line into 5 or 10 year segments up to your present age.

Using the marks of ages and years, make notations for yourself at the points in life where you are aware of beginnings and endings.

These transitional points are *initiations* into new ways of being. They are the opening of Life Chapters and closing of Life Chapters. They represent the ebb and flow, life/death/life cycle, over and over again.

Look over your life line and see if you've completed your many life transitions—if you've closed life chapters cleanly and opened others knowingly. Be sure to celebrate and/or consciously experience your life transitions.

THE BIGGER PICTURE

In one of many remarkable interviews, acclaimed television journalist Bill Moyers asked Joseph Campbell, renowned scholar, and author of mythology and life, "Do you have faith?" Campbell laughed and said, "I don't need faith, I have experience."

In the beginning of life, you need faith; you don't have experience for reference. After enough years of experience (I'd say between 35 and 40), you can finally begin to identify the rhythms, cycles and "loops" of experience of your life. You can begin to trust your process more, through personal knowing. I've felt, and have said for years, that "I was born 35 and that it felt great to catch up." It's great to finally *fit into myself*. The opportunity to appreciate the bigger picture is wonderful.

So, depending on your age, you will have short or long "life

*Sometimes I go about
pitying myself,
and all the time
I am being carried
on great winds across the sky.*

Ojibway Saying

histories" to review in the Life Line graph that you create from the exercise above. And like Joseph Campbell, you will have experience, the helicopter's view, that is needed to detach from conditioned beliefs and programmed responses. Experience helps rid us of the anxious, usually guilt-ridden, condemning mental chatter that obscures the view of the puzzle. Seeing the bigger picture can help us to grasp how it's all been working together all along, teaching us lessons and guiding us in certain directions, no matter how much kicking and screaming we've done along the way!

There is a soul force in the universe, which, if we permit it, will flow through us and produce miraculous results.

Mahatma Gandhi

Chapter 19

STAGE 11: ReDecision

*The real voyage of discovery
consists not in seeking new landscapes
but in having new eyes.*

Marcel Proust

BACK TO THE FUTURE—YOU MADE IT!

CONGRATULATIONS! Breathe. Sigh. Relax. You've made it. You're home free. "How could I ever have even thought of being, doing or having it the other way?" You've made a ReDecision! (Figure 29) You've let go of the outdated belief, the conditioned mental model, and now, shift, you have a new belief. You've come full circle, back to a "new normal."

One of the greatest self-management tools you have is to choose to redecide—to make a choice. Your redecision seems like the right way and the only way it should ever have been done. We sometimes forget our struggle. We forget the doubt and fear. We forget the original questions. That's all right. This, too, shall pass!

TOUCHSTONE:
If you're alive, you'll get another chance to grow and change. Soon.

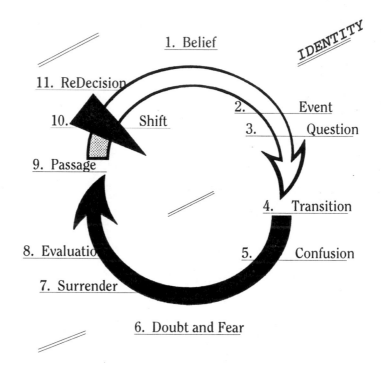

Figure 29 The ReDecisions 11-Stage Model - STAGE 11

RENEWAL

Although it may seem that we live life in a linear fashion, we do not. Life proceeds in a spiral of growth and change. Have you ever found yourself thinking, "Haven't I gone through this before?" or "You'd think I would have learned this by now." Hopefully, every loop of the spiral reflects continued improvement and a higher consciousness of the world and our life choices. Over time, we learn the Life Lesson and let go of some of the experiences. We will not live them again. Others may return again and again, until we "get it"...or not.

THE UPWARD SPIRAL

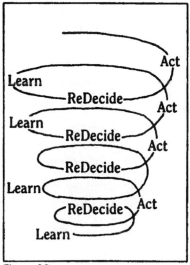

Figure 30

*To see your drama clearly is
to be liberated from it.*

Ken Keyes, Jr.
*Handbook to
Higher Consciousness*

Life in a continuing spiral: *Learn - ReDecide - Act*. This cycle takes us to each higher plane of life and living, as we put the energy into moving and into changing. Learn - ReDecide - Act, Learn - ReDecide - Act. Over and over again. You cannot have any one of these without the others. If you think you can, plan on spending some time in more confusion and frustration.

All of life is about growing and changing, moving from one mental model to the next. We renew ourselves inside and out through being consciously open to the letting go of blocks, limits and old mindsets that do not serve us. The greatest risk in this process is losing the self (that is already breaking away, anyway) and letting the new Self evolve.

We don't create our lives nor do we ever really set or meet goals. We are, all along, only letting our lives unfold to what they are to be. It's like we chose a great and perfect life path and experience before we were born; then after birth, we forgot it and buried it under others' conditioning and programmed direction.

TOUCHSTONE:
We are here each moment to re-member.

The more open we are to newness, and to *getting out of our own way*, the more the unfolding seems like magic, miracles, luck and

*When a man's willing
and eager,
the gods join in.*

Aeschylus
Greek dramatist

serendipity. Our job, then, is to open our minds and hearts to the big picture of life, to set our goals (steps toward our desires and vision) and take action. The unfolding (including all of those "coincidences" and "accidents") may not match our picture exactly, but for many willing to risk this way of life, it can take us farther than we ever thought possible. The new normals will seem incredible. The new mental models will be amazing. This is the way it's *supposed* to be. *This* is normal!

TOUCHSTONE:
Every ending is a beginning, and every beginning, an end.
Every death is a birth, and every birth, a death.

EXERCISE:
List redecisions you have made in the past month, year, five years and lifetime. How did it feel to make the shift and redecide?

List areas of your life that you would like to redecide in the next month, year, five years and lifetime. Sentence starters might be:
1. I'd like to . . .
2. I'd *really* like to . . .
3. I'd *REALLY* like to . . .
4. I wish that I could . . .
5. I want to . . .
6. I wish I didn't have to . . .
7. I will . . .

In a nutshell, the process of growth is:
❦   Set goals (listen to yourself - trust your inner voice)
❦   Ask questions
❦   Make choices
❦   Take action
❦   Evaluate outcomes
❦   ReDecide where needed
❦   Start all over again
❦   Honor and respect yourself and your needs
❦   Enhance your self-image, self-esteem and self-confidence with healthy, positive life choices
❦   Live life fully
❦   Don't get attached to the outcomes

TOUCHSTONE:
You're not here for a long time, you're here for a good time!

Life is a series of natural and
spontaneous changes.
Don't resist them—
that only creates sorrow.
Let reality be reality.
Let things flow naturally forward
in whatever way they like.

Lao-Tse

VII

---••●•••---

The Lessons

---••●•••---

*Without a task that challenges,
there can be no transformation.
Without a task there is no real sense of satisfaction.
To love pleasure takes little.
To love truly takes a hero who can manage his own fear.*

Clarissa Pinkola Estés
Women Who Run With the Wolves

*The highest reward for a person's toil
is not what they get for it,
but what they become by it.*

John Ruskin

Chapter 20

THE BLACK HOLE

Denial is not a River in Egypt.

Coffee mug

❧

Let's now expand on what happens between Stage 9: Passage and Stage 10: Mental Model Shift, when the shift is not made—The Black Hole (Figure 32).

In Chapter 17 I described three forks in the road at the passage. Either you move into and through Stage 10, the Mental Model Shift, and on to redecide your new belief (FORKS 1 or 2) or, for whatever reason, you hold onto your old belief (FORK 3). The three paths, again, are:

FORK 1: Mental Model Shift.
> You get the "Oh!", creating a mental model shift to move on to ReDecide, a new belief and new identity.

FORK 2: ReCommit.
> You get the "Oh!", creating a mental model shift that recognizes, in fact, that your old belief *was* right. You choose from an "Action-ary," conscious menu and ReCommit to your belief.

FORK 3: Black Hole.
> You decide that your intuition, inner guidance and everyone else's support and help is wrong.   Change is too

uncomfortable and you are not going to change even though it will be worse than before and is not healthy. You stop and ReTurn.

Why would we choose the third path? Why would we consciously choose to be in the Black Hole? FORK 3 is known by many names: denial, delusion, false pride, ego, fear and stubbornness, just to name a few. But no matter what it is called, it feels like *hell*.

THE PATH OF FORK 3
USING THE REDECISIONS MODEL

Here is an example of someone moving through the complete cycle of each of the stages in the ReDecisions 11-Stage Model. The italicized words from the model stages will take you easily through the process.

A person, I'll call him Tom, has had a lot of feedback throughout his life regarding his drinking. Tom, however, *believes* that he is fine. His *identity* about himself is that he doesn't have a problem. He believes that everyone else (they) has the problem (blame, denial, delusion). Then, one day, an *event* happens. Tom gets picked up for drunk driving. Through this event process, he *questions* his drinking, thinking and behavior. Tom begins a *transition*. He begins to "see" himself and his mindset differently.

Tom feels *confused* and frustrated. He realizes what it can mean to him to change his belief about his drinking. This will change his whole identity, his friends, the way he spends his time, money, energy, his rituals and routines. He moves into *doubt and fear*, grief and loss. He feels anger and depression about changing a lifestyle that he believes is okay (denial, delusion).

Finally, through soul searching and other pressures from family, friends and the court system, Tom *surrenders*. He accepts that he has a problem and that he will work on changing himself. He slowly starts to *trust* the process and gains *hope* for a new way of living that will be better in all areas of life. He *evaluates* his options and decides, through feedback and information from education on alcohol abuse and addiction, that maybe it's time for a change. He begins his *passage* into a *mental model shift* (FORK 1: "Oh!") that will take him into a *redecision* about himself and his new belief that will offer him a healthier lifestyle, and possibly, his life.

But even with all the education—Alcoholics Anonymous meetings, books, tapes, support, prayers, pressure and purpose—Tom decides to drink again. He gets caught in the abyss, the shaded area between Stages 9 and 10, the *Black Hole*, FORK 3 (Figure 31).

And in all of my experience, I have never seen lasting solutions to problems, lasting happiness and success, that came from the outside in.

Stephen Covey
The Seven Habits of Highly Effective People

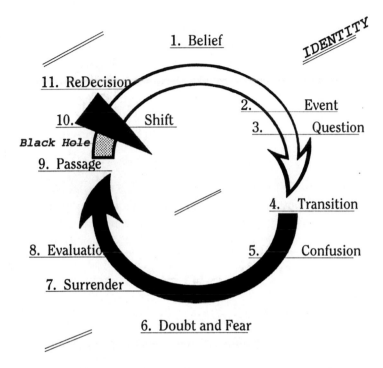

Figure 31 The ReDecisions 11-Stage Model - The Black Hole

The real problem? Not that Tom is drinking again, which could ultimately cost him everything, but that now Tom is drinking *consciously*. He "knows too much." In the past, Tom drank in ignorance. For the most part, he lived unconsciously, versus now, drinking in guilt, shame and fear. The Black Hole.

HABIT

Have you ever experienced life in the Black Hole? We don't have to go to such painful lengths in the story of Tom to find examples of this experience in each of our daily lives. After each of the following questions, whether you answer yes or no, be aware of your feelings about your answer.

- 🕊 Did you exercise today, this week, this year?
- 🕊 Do you eat a healthy diet?
- 🕊 Are you overweight or underhealthy?
- 🕊 Did you spend money you don't have on things you don't need?
- 🕊 Do you hold resentments, anger or blame toward another?

Everything, even darkness and silence has its wonders.

Helen Keller

> • Do you spend appropriate and positive time with your family?
> • Add your own.

Do you find yourself feeling guilty, ashamed, wrong or bad because you haven't been paying attention to some of these life areas? Do you hear yourself justify and rationalize your answers? Each of us, on a daily basis, has gone through Stages 1-8, reading, researching, hearing all the statistics and learning all the answers. We get ready to change and...no passage, no shift. We continue to do it "the same old way," but now consciously, with guilt, paranoia and self-loathing. *Hell.*

"It's habit," you argue. "It's not *that* big of a deal. It's not that bad *yet*. I'll change *later*." Supporting habits, patterns and other conditioned thinking and behaving only imbeds them deeper into our mental model system. It's no easier to change later and, in some situations, it will be too late.

PROJECTION

Why is this important? Our perceptions of ourselves and how we believe others perceive us defines our self-image. This ultimately effects our self-esteem, self-respect, self-confidence and feelings of worth and deservedness in the world. This, remember, then becomes *our* projection, our shadow—we dump on others and the world every day. You kick the dog, the dog bites the cat....

This story may illustrate this point even more clearly. You are in a movie theater and don't like the movie. You go up and rip the movie screen off the wall to stop the movie. Does it stop? Of course not. Why not? The movie doesn't come from the screen, it comes from the projector. More specifically, it comes from the light passing through the *film* in the projector.

This is how we tend to view the world. Whenever we don't like something or someone, we want *them* or *it* to change, then we'd feel better. *They* may not change and even if *it* did, it doesn't mean you'd feel any better. The problem isn't *out there* on the movie screen of life. It's *in here*, in the projector—your movie film mindset of conditioned perceptions and beliefs running in your head and out your lens—eyes, ears and other senses.

Whether we relate to our minds and thoughts as being like a movie film or like the disks in a computer, we are responsible for the pictures, sounds, messages, ratings, bytes, input, output and upkeep of our system. As adults we have the right and the responsibility to EDIT, DELETE and CUT out any and all conditioned pieces of information and learning that is outdated, unhealthy, old and limiting.

The more conscious we choose to be on a continual basis, the more easily we will be able to EDIT more quickly and move through the passage into the shift. Of course, feel free to linger in the Black Hole at times; it's okay, but don't sign a lease.

CHANGE—SLOW BUT SURE

Are there times when we know we need to change but it just doesn't feel like it's time, or it feels too overwhelming? Yes. Sometimes it is not realistically possible to change all the issues you are dealing with at once. Like a garden that has not been kept up, tilled and planted for years and has gone to weeds, it will take a while to create it into a beautiful, wonderful environment again, or for the first time. When we let our conditioning (weeds) take over our lives (gardens) for a long time, it's not going to change overnight. But you can start on one or two areas that you feel you can get a handle on; again, like dominos, they will start to affect all other areas that need weeding.

When we *know too much* and don't risk the leap into the new identity, we fall back into fear, frustration and limited perspective. So, the answer is, "Don't learn anything new so that you don't know and it can't hurt you!" EHHHH! WRONG ANSWER. Life will always offer you answers. Your inner voice tends to nag at you, anyway, even though you find ways to mindlessly run from it.

TOUCHSTONE:
We can put off and escape taking action, but we can't escape knowing.

GUILT

We do have a choice over how we feel about our behaviors. I'm not saying we should be sociopathic and go do anything we want with no guilt. But the average human being, including you and me, wastes a lot of time and energy feeling guilty, worrying, feeling anxious and stressed out over what we know we should do and shouldn't do, but don't do either.

TOUCHSTONE:
Either do it or don't do it, but don't feel guilty.

*Do you want to be right
or do you want to be well?*

Attributed to Dr. Karl Menninger

*Our options are to learn
this new game, the rules, the
roles of the participants and
how the rewards are distributed,
or to continue practicing our
present skills and
become the best players
in a game that is
no longer being played.*

Larry Wilson
*Changing the Game:
The New Way to Sell*

If, for instance, you're trying to lose weight, and you find yourself sneaking ice cream, *stop sneaking*. Sneaking anything is like lying and being dishonest, it is a shame-based activity, creating paranoia, guilt and more shame. Either eat it or don't eat it, but don't get caught in the middle—eating out of the carton standing at the freezer. Scoop some ice cream into a bowl or a cone, play couch potato for a while and really enjoy your feast. The act of sneaking sets up more mental models of being wrong and bad, self-criticism, regrets, remorse and such. Who needs it?

EXERCISE:
In order to get out of feeling guilt and despair over unrealistic expectations and lack of healthy boundaries, write a list of all the things you feel that you "should," "ought to," "must," "have to," "need to" and "want to" do.

Go through this list marking the following two items:

1. Mark any item that is *not* yours to be doing. It's someone else's need or should or want and *somehow* it got on your list. Delegate it back to the person, and vow to stop taking on other's needs. Going the extra mile once in a while is a good thing, but not all the time.

2. Make a check mark for those things that really are *your* items to do and that, if you do them, make your life better. Take charge of these checked items and make a plan to accomplish them in a timely manner. By doing the things *you really* need, want or have to do, you will feel better for their completion and less frustrated for having eliminated from your list all the things you don't need or want to do.

The Black Hole is the great abyss of life where we either take the leap or backpedal. It is a painful place filled with wagging index fingers, shame, blame, fear and guilt. When you hear yourself blaming others or yourself, and using words like *should, have to, better, ought to, must, always* and *never,* you can be assured that you are in the Black Hole. Only you can move yourself out and past the Black Hole. You alone can take your own leap.

Courage is the price that Life exacts for granting peace.

Amelia Earhart

EXERCISE:
Make a list of the areas of your life that you would like to change,

things that you would like to be different. This may differ from the previous list. For each, write down what you can do about it to change it, to make the shift happen.

Next to each listing, make a check mark for those things you are willing to do something about in the next month for proactive change. Be honest; only check those that you truly are going to do something about. Make a plan. Write it down. Set a schedule for follow-through and go for it.

What about those that you did not check? Let them go. Next month, go through your list again and reevaluate if you are ready to work on another one or two on your list. If not, that's okay, too.

Either way, choose not to feel guilty, wrong or bad about not acting on changing something you "know you should work on." Do at least one thing toward one of the items. That may be the domino that fells all the rest. You have to start somewhere.

TOUCHSTONE:
Stop "shoulding" on yourself.

When you feel that you have reached the end and that you cannot go one step further, when life seems to be drained of all purpose: What a wonderful opportunity to start all over again to turn over a new page.

Eileen Caddy
Footprints on the Path

> *Just as water clarifies when you allow it to settle,*
> *the same is true with the mind.*
>
> Lama Sogyal Rinpoche

Chapter 21

A TIME TO GROW,
A TIME TO REST

Sometimes we need to stop growing.
We may need to backstep and regress.

Thomas Moore
Care of the Soul

One of my favorite cartoons that addresses the issue of *resting* on our path is one by Gail Machlis, *Quality Time*. A man and a woman are at a singles' gathering. The man leans over to the woman and says, "I can't tell you what a pleasure it is to talk with someone who isn't on a spiritual quest."

Do you ever get tired of growing and changing? Depending on who you are, where you live and the people you associate with, you may find that there's hardly a sentence that's spoken that doesn't involve personal growth, self-development, spiritual journey or the like. With all of my travel, there are times that I look forward to trips to parts of the country where the discussions center around topics like crops and weather and the crops and weather. It's refreshing, and I find it helps me to literally "ground" myself in a very different way. I know that I need to stop, rest, retreat and reset often, too.

*A teacher, if indeed wise,
does not bid you
to enter the house of their
wisdom, but leads you to the
threshold of your own mind.*

Kahlil Gibran
Poet and Painter (1883-1931)

SHORT CUT REDECISIONS

It is important to understand that we do not go through all 11 stages of the ReDecisions Model every time we change a belief. Going through the "dark night of the soul" experience is clearly for those transitions in life where we question deep seated mental models. These mindsets are the core of our life, our identity, and take time, work and pain to move them out.

Other less rooted beliefs and mindsets change more easily. In this case, you will most likely skip Stage 6: Doubt and Fear, moving quickly through questioning, confusion and surrender into a shift for your redecision. We do this daily with ongoing decisions about work and family and how to spend our time and energy. We weigh the pros and cons of options available and make decisions constantly. It is a natural ebb and flow.

STOP. REST.

It's okay to stop and rest. Be conscious of being *too* conscious at times. Just hang out and "be" more often. Whatever is going to come into your life to ask you to question your beliefs will come along anyway. If you are *mindfully* hanging around, proactively "being," an event will happen, and you will think, "Oh, look at this—an event. I see it's time to work on something." (I trust that you will say it just like that, too!)

In 1978, as an undergraduate practicum student, I spent two semesters training as a counselor at a chemical dependency inpatient treatment center. One day, after being there for several months, Clay and Kenny, two of the counselors there, challenged me. They confronted me saying that I was the most controlling person they'd ever met and giving numerous examples of this behavior. And, furthermore, that I couldn't be spontaneous. Well, I took them up on that challenge. I argued that I *did too* know how to be spontaneous and would *prove* it to them. At which point I took out my day-timer (here's a clue) and scheduled in "SPONTANEITY" for the next Saturday from 2-3 P.M.. When Saturday came around, my ego and unconscious conditioned beliefs had to "eat crow." Of course, I could have eaten crow the moment I reached for my day-timer. But, Clay and Kenny let me go another couple of days thinking I knew who I was!

Stop, rest, relax.

LIFE LESSONS IN THE SCHOOL OF LIFE

Because we are all enrolled in The School of Life, and it is just a series of Life Lessons, we have opportunities on an ongoing basis to let go, detach and to make redecisions. The following (Figure 32) illustrates this point.

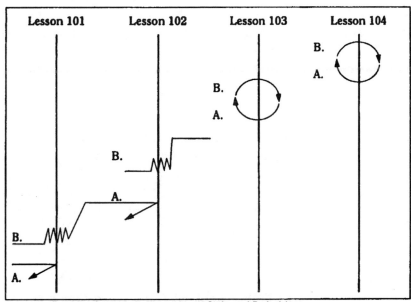

Figure 32 Ongoing Life Lessons, Mental Model Shifts and Redecisions

Suppose this illustration covers the Lessons for taking the risk of being more assertive in your job. Life Lesson 101-A represents the path of taking the courage to make the "leap," request the raise, ask for your needs to be met or whatever the issue might be. You move toward the event, and you stop. You don't do it. You back down. You find it's not worth it, it's not that important right now or that you're just too afraid to follow through. You may fear what others will think of you, fear the conflict or rejection, fear the loss of security and safety or others.

You will notice, in Figure 32, that you will not be able to move from Life Lesson 101 and go on to Life Lesson 102 until you leap *through* the experience, gaining the cellular "Oh!" that will change you forever—moving you up the spiral.

TOUCHSTONE:
Sometimes you "can't *not* do it."

Let's now examine Life Lesson 101-B. This lesson represents the path of taking the information and courage that you have to make the "leap," request the raise, ask for your needs to be met or whatever the issue, and *you leap*. You do it. You find that it was not

Life loves to be taken by the lapel and be told: "I am with you, kid. Let's go."

Maya Angelou

only the time to take the risk and follow through, but that possibly it was even more uncomfortable *not* doing it than doing it. It was worth dealing with any conflict or other issues of fear that came up for you to have pushed *through* the passage and the shift.

Every cell in your body gets the "Oh!" You did it! (Enter *Rocky* theme song). The accordion line across LL101-B illustrates shaking of knees, sweaty palms and chattering teeth. It's probably never going to be easy. *That's why they're called Lessons.* It's something to learn. You are the student.

Now that you've risked—you may not get what you asked for. Did you gather all of your courage and ask for a raise, just to get turned down? Possibly. You still win. You did the work. The Lesson wasn't about getting the raise, it was about *risking to ask for it*—meaning risking to develop your self-esteem and self-confidence to this new level (More *Rocky* theme song).

You can now go on to Life Lesson 102, where you meet a new challenge, a different situation. And so goes life from birth, to death, to birth. Another Lesson design will be for another life area: money management, assertiveness, physical health, relationships, trusting yourself and so on.

Life is but an endless series of experiments.

Mahatma Gandhi

Notice LL103 and LL104 in Figure 32. These show the ReDecisions Model arrows at the intersection of the Lesson and you. Each Life Lesson is a point of decision, challenge, choice and redecision, the entire redecisions process over and over again. Some go quickly, others take time.

A TIME FOR REST

In between the Lessons there is rest time. It is fruitless to try to do everything at once. Your body, psyche, spirit and soul need time to incubate, percolate and integrate the new information.

In order to study ahead in the Life Lesson series, it is helpful to evaluate all life areas on an ongoing basis to see what you want and what you don't want. As life invites you to participate in its Lessons, looking ahead can help you feel a little more in charge, in the flow, of the process.

TOUCHSTONE:
THE BAD NEWS is that setting goals and getting specific about how you want your life to look will bring even more Life Lessons to you.
THE GOOD NEWS is that setting goals and getting specific about how you want your life to look will bring even more Life Lessons to you.

RE-SETTING LIFE GOALS
The best way to learn the ebb and flow of action and rest in life is to proactively set goals. If we are not actively seeking our purpose and in forward movement, we are bobbing up and down in the ocean like a buoy, controlled by outside movement and direction. If you are not "unfolding" into life, you stay stuck, *folded*. This is *not* rest, this is a setup for living out the victim-martyr helpless role.

True goal setting will help you take charge of your "movement" and your "rest" on an ongoing basis.

Autumn . . .
makes demands . . .
that we learn to let go—
to acknowledge the beauty
of sparseness.

Bonaro W. Overstreet

EXERCISE:
In a spiral notebook, give each of the following 15 life/work goal setting areas several pages each for writing your wants, needs and aspirations.

For each goal area make the following two columns:
"What I DON'T Want," and "What I DO Want."

1.   Emotional/Feelings
2.   Professional - Vocation/Career/Job
3.   Financial/Money Management
4.   Spiritual
5.   Health: Physical/Nutritional
6.   Personal Growth: Mental/Intellectual/Educational
7.   Family
8.   Interactional: Personal Relationships/Social
9.   Community Support/Involvement
10. Sensual/Sexual
11. Personal Environment: Living Space/Neighborhood
12.   Who/What I Want to *Be*
13. Things I Want to *Do*
14. Things I Want to *Have*

15. Other/Miscellaneous

Be sure to ask yourself:
❧ What do YOU *really* want?
❧ What are YOU willing to create?

When you're writing your lists, start with what you don't want and write them down. This helps to identify them, to let them go and to get them out of your mind and your thoughts. Then write in the list of what you do want. Over time, it will be normal to mentally note your "don't wants", being aware of them and dismissing them quickly, and moving on to your do wants.

TAKE TIME TO PROCESS

From your *"DO* Want" list you can continue to create your pro-active life choices. As you expand, add and subtract from your list over your lifetime, note that part of your goal development is to plan time to rest. Making conscious choices and scheduling time to rest in between action steps, taking "process time" is as important as the action steps themselves.

TOUCHSTONE:
Destiny is not a matter of chance, it is a matter of choice.

Everything you ask for and pray for, believe that you have it already and it will be yours.

Jesus Christ (0-33 A.D.)
Mark 11:24
The Bible

Have you ever set a goal, achieved it and then didn't want it? As an added piece of goal setting information, I find it very helpful after stating any goal to say, "This or something better." Why? We have very finite minds. We don't always know what is best for us. Our job is to set our goals and take action toward them. "How" it ends up looking may be slightly or completely different than we had imagined. Experience has taught me that it is usually greater and better than we could have ever dreamed, even when it's not exactly what we thought it would be. And, you can almost always change it - again.

TOUCHSTONE:
Watch out for what you pray/wish for. You'll get it and may not want it.

BE SPECIFIC

A note here on being as specific as possible when setting goals. Back when I didn't know who I was and what I wanted in many areas of my life, I read a book on creative visualization and imagery. This book was a guide about how to control my mental movie, the pictures I see in my head, to be clear about what I wanted in life and to then move toward it in a clear and focused manner.

Because I tend to "skim" books when I read, I got the part about seeing in your mind's eye exactly what you want and affirming that it was true. At the time, I hadn't been dating anyone for a while and decided I would put energy into this area. I affirmed, "I see hundreds of men in my life." I "saw" myself being in relationships and put a lot of mind power and sincere emotional energy into it.

Well, it worked! Within two months, I got what I had asked for. My next job title was Director of Counseling at Salvation Army Men's Rehabilitation Center. Okay, laugh, but I got *exactly* what I asked for—hundreds of men. It was a *100-bed facility*. If I had been more *specific*, it might have looked different.

Being general with goal setting is like calling Sears and Roebuck catalog department and saying, "Send me something you think I'd like."

Rev. Edwene Gaines

EXERCISE:
Think of one goal you are striving for. Write down all of the specifics that you can think of for that goal. If you find yourself being general about it, don't be surprised when what you create is general.

Fear of success, again, is the culprit for not being specific. "What if I get what I ask for and don't want it?" Well, outside of children (you can't put them back), there are very few goals that cannot be returned, taken back, realized and released for the identified more specific and perfect creation for you. Remember: "This or something better." You deserve it.

STOP SCARING YOURSELF!

I overheard an elderly man talking about winning the lottery, or wishes of it, as he waited for the numbers to be read on television. He was standing holding a lottery ticket and stated, "I hope I don't win." I asked him why he'd say such a thing. He answered, "I don't know what I'd do with all that money. How could you ever spend that much? I'd probably have a heart attack, we'd have to move because people would be jealous of us, and you know somebody would probably kidnap our grandkids for ransom...." Facinating! I told him that I had plenty of ideas for the money, so, if he was going to die of a heart attack after winning, I wanted to be close by and know where that ticket landed!

Wisdom doesn't automatically come with old age. Nothing does— except wrinkles. It's true, some wines improve with age. But only if the grapes were good in the first place.

Abigail Van Buren
Dear Abby

THE FOUR RULES FOR LIVING

Here is another tip—the following are the simple, yet deeply profound, Four Rules For Living, written by cultural anthropologist Angeles Arrien.

These few points say everything about Life Lessons and our need to weave in and out of our life experience the understanding that no matter what is happening—it too shall change, and we can handle it.

1. Show up
2. Pay attention
3. Tell the truth
4. Don't be attached to the results

*This is the mechanism
of consciousness:
whenever you live something
consciously it never becomes a
loaded thing on you. It never
becomes a burden on you
if you live it consciously.
Whatever you live
unconsciously becomes a
hangover, because you never live
it totally—something
remains incomplete.
When something is incomplete it
has to be carried—
it waits to be completed.*

Osho
Article, *Unburden the Memory*

Chapter 22

INTELLECT, INSIGHT AND WISDOM

*Each dark night and every little death
peels away a layer of conditioning,
restoring our sight so that
we can apprehend reality more clearly.*

Joan Borysenko

Our life experiences can bring us vast measures of Intellect, we "think" more clearly; Insight, we "see" more clearly; and Wisdom, we "know" more deeply than we ever did before (Figure 33).

INTELLECT

Over and over again in life we come out of the *dark underworld* into the *light upperworld* with a new knowing, information and education. Our experience has helped us to attain mental Intellect.

Intellectually trying to explain our dark night of the soul to others may be another story. Have you ever started talking about your experience through one of these times to someone, and they either laugh it off or give you that look that says "Hey. Stop now. You're *out there!*" You alone have had your exact experience. There are many others, though, who will listen because they realize the importance of going down and coming back up alive, and returning even better than before the journey. Do seek them out.

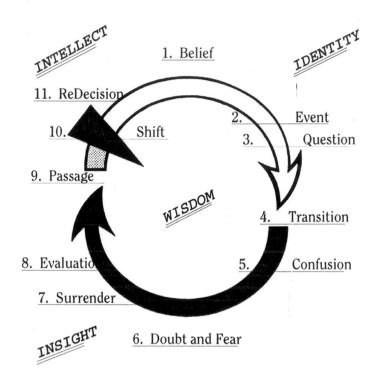

Figure 33 The ReDecisions 11-Stage Model

INSIGHT

Insight can bring us "Heaven." As we "get" the Life Lessons we are drawn to learn, insight helps us see the bigger picture and shift into our new way of thinking and being.

Many people, however, forgo insight in the underworld experience, the hard times and work of change, heart and soul emotional experience, for intellect, a head experience. They push it away, make it unimportant, and miss the *depth* of the learning experience. Our modern world does not serve us well to understand and work through the process of transition, the gap in continuity of existence. For many people, emptiness and times of change, endings and completions represent only the *absence* of something. So when the *something* is as important as relatedness and purpose, transformation and reality, we try to find ways of replacing these missing elements as quickly as possible.[33] Unfortunately, then, the void, the dark night experience, is not seen as an important part of the transition process—it is only a temporary state of loss to be endured. And *enduring* is not a key to accessing the lesson to be learned.

Insight is gained by *being* in the dark, empty times. By feeling and experiencing the process, this emptiness can give us perspective in and of our lives that no other time can offer. It is here that we can see what is meant by the statement "Everything is illusion," making our everyday world look transparent and insubstantial.

My friend Bill found that how he needed to deal with this experience of loss and frustration was to enjoy it. Bill was laid off of two computer programmer jobs within 20 months. The first time, he fought it, trying to get the next job, worrying about money and such, and literally making himself ill over it. The second time it happened, due to his prior experience, he learned that he could handle it—he "got it." Bill detached, he decided not to waste time on stressing himself out. He did his work applying for jobs, but this time rested, enjoying his new home (purchased just before the first layoff), his wife and some "time off." He was rehired soon after.

We can't live in the underworld long, it would kill us. But every time we go there, empty out and remake ourselves, we bring back to the "real" world an appreciation of the unknowable ground beyond every image— beyond our mental models and limits.

Many such experiences over a lifetime produce wisdom.

WISDOM

You've probably known people who have gone through major life transitions, even took the leap and shifted. But they must have missed the wisdom part. As noted earlier, when something is this important and anxiety provoking, we try to find ways of replacing these missing elements as quickly as possible; we try to *endure it*. Just to endure it would be bad enough, but there are many who go outside of themselves to find a "fix" for the problem. Alcohol, drugs (legal and illegal), food, work, sex, even therapy, are ways people run from themselves, to make "it" go away.

We don't gain wisdom simply by enduring and, needless to say, not from the above mentioned "fixes." We gain wisdom by being *a part of the process* in our own lives. Like the story of Bill, I've heard people state in remorse about positive or interesting events of the past, "Why didn't I enjoy it when I was there?" Or, "I wish I had taken the time to stop and really work through it when I had the chance." Well, all of life is the same, wisdom comes from "being" in your life.

LIVING MINDFULLY

Dr. Shelley Taylor, a UCLA-based psychologist studying people whose lives had been disrupted by misfortunes that ranged from rape to life-threatening illnesses, found that those who readjusted

*All truly wise thoughts
have been thought already
thousands of times;
but to make them truly ours,
we must think them
over again honestly,
till they take root in
our personal experience.*

Johann Wolfgang von Goethe

well incorporated three coping strategies into their recoveries:
1. A search for meaning in the experience,
2. An attempt to gain mastery over the event in particular and life in general, and
3. A recouping of self-esteem after they had suffered some loss or setback.

She found that the meaning we ascribe to these dark nights of the soul, the wisdom that we can glean from crisis and pain and take back into the world as intellect and insight, is central to how we emerge from them.[34]

Rather than folding in times of crisis, most people have the innate capacity to recover from monumental problems, readjusting to life not only as well as, but even better than, before the tragedy occurred. Some people call their tragic life events gifts, blessings and "Perfect. Exactly what was to happen." These people lived mindfully "through" the transition, gaining compassion for their life journey and clarity for their overall life experience as it relates to this "rude awakening" on the path.

Through our experience of our fears, pain and confusion, it is in wisdom we can gain *compassion* for ourselves and for others. Taking this compassion, openness and flexibility back with us into our *intellect*ual daily lives makes life more livable for everyone.

COMING HOME
After all is said and done, is this whole thing worth it? Well...
a) You don't have a choice about going through the process; if you're alive, it's going to happen, and
b) You do have a choice whether to be conscious throughout it or not.

As we learn to be more flexible and aware in our movement through these stages, we begin to appreciate the change and transformation it offers us. We move from our "self," our everyday, human, routine and finite frame of mind, to realizing our "Self," that higher, creative core-being that we really are, but through conditioned beliefs, we have lost. All of life is a journey of *coming home to your Self*, the reuniting with oneself, wholeness and connection.

We are very empty inside,
just watch us work
to fill up the vacant hours.

Sujata
Beginning to See

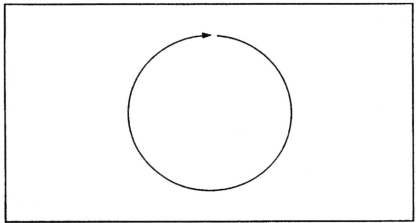

Figure 34 Loop back to self

According to one modern psychologist, the late Abraham Maslow, this process of transition, shifts and redecisions is paramount to our growth, well-being and transformation. In the process, we become what he termed "self-actualized."

To be a person who connects with and lives this higher Self-nature, self-actualization, more often and more consistently is what Abraham Maslow wrote about in his landmark book *Toward A Psychology of Being*.

> We may define it as an episode, or a spurt in which the powers of the person come together in a particularly efficient and intensely enjoyable way, and in which he is more integrated and less split, more open for experience, more idiosyncratic, more perfectly expressive or spontaneous, or fully functioning, more creative, more humorous, more ego-transcending, more independent of his lower needs, etc. He becomes in these episodes more truly himself, more perfectly actualizing his potentialities, closer to the core of his Being, more fully human.[35]

*We must not cease
from exploration.
And the end of all our exploring
will be to arrive
where we began
and to know the place
for the first time.*

T.S. Eliot

*The seeker is that
which is being sought.*

Buddhist saying

*Before enlightenment
chopping wood
carrying water.
After enlightenment
chopping wood
carrying water.*

Zen proverb

Be not a slave of your own past—
plunge into the sublime seas,
dive deep,
and swim far,
so you shall come back
with self-respect, with new power,
and an advanced experience,
that shall explain
and overlook the old.

Ralph Waldo Emerson

EXERCISE:
Think back over a major transition in your life. What did you learn and gain about yourself and life on each of the following three levels?

1. INTELLECT
   "Oh!"
2. INSIGHT
   "Oh! - Yeah."
3. WISDOM
   "Oh! - Mmmm."

The lesson, the insight and wisdom you gain through any experience (experienced mindfully) will move you up the evolutionary ladder, supporting you through your next redecisions process. Always take time out to feel and integrate the changes and deeply realize the shifts so that they become an integral and supportive part of who you are and your everyday life.

MICHELANGELO AND ANGEL

It is said that when a passerby approached Michelangelo, who was chipping an angel out of a block of marble, he remarked, "Oh, Michelangelo you are creating such a beautiful angel." Michelangelo replied, "No, I'm just helping the angel out. He's been in here all along." And so it is the same for each of us.

TOUCHSTONE:
It is our self's job to bring out our Self.

No one can give you wisdom.
You must discover it
for yourself,
on the journey through life,
which no one can take for you.

Sun Bear

Figure 35 Michelangelo and the Angel

> *There is an amazing great and brilliant light*
> *in the center of the black hole in the universe.*
> *They are the grinding down of stars into gases and dust,*
> *swirling and compressing*
> *with such great pressure and speed*
> *that light is formed.*
>
> Stephen Hawking
> *Stephen Hawking's Universe*

Chapter 23

LIFE'S TOO SHORT NOT TO LIVE IT

⁂

Since everything is but an apparition,
perfect in being what it is,
having nothing to do with good or bad,
acceptance or rejection
one may well burst out in laughter.

Long Chen Pa
Tibetan Meditation Master

⁂

QUESTION EVERYTHING — TRUST YOURSELF

So, does all of this make sense? We end and begin, and begin and end, over and over again from birth until death. That is life. Living life fully, consciously, keeps us in constant motion on the upward evolutionary spiral of life. Because of free will, we can choose to stop growing, causing pain and frustration on all levels, or we can choose to keep growing, causing fear, anxiety, excitement, surprises and many positive reactions.

Studies show that only five percent of the population even thinks about taking the first step: waking up, becoming aware and setting goals. Taking charge of your life means acting on your intuition, guts, hunches, experience, knowledge, education, vision and common sense. It is trusting that the new door will open when the old one has closed. It is being willing to not step back when the void is darker and deeper than you could have expected. It is learning to question everything and to trust yourself.

LIGHTEN UP!

What about humor throughout all of this? Yes, you'd better learn to laugh —a lot. Last year, part of my dark night experience included several surgeries and hospitalizations. One hospital visit required two different doctors for different surgical needs. I decided that I was not going to make myself crazy over this whole thing, so as I went into the operating room, I took with me several copies of funny cartoons about hospital care that I had clipped from the paper. That way, everyone working on me and with me had at least a running start at lightening up while I was *out*.

For the doctors, I had a special letter. I welcomed them to a great day with hopes that they had their "go juice" for the morning. I also noted that "The next time I'm naked with two men and have to pay them, I'm going to be awake and enjoy it!"

At 75, Dorothy, a friend of mine, has been widowed three times and never married to anyone longer than seven years. She looks back over her life remembering the deaths and losses of husbands: her first husband was a test pilot for the National Guard—after making it through WWII, he was killed in an airplane crash at 33; her second husband died a sudden death at 36 from a blood clot through the heart; and her last husband died at 55 of a massive heart attack after years of rheumatic fever. How has she gotten through her grief? "I had to learn to laugh at life and at myself."

LIVE LIFE FULLY

If we wait for the big exciting things in life to happen "someday when..." we may miss out on a lot of life. My friend Ruth's 3 year old daughter Elissa asked me if I could put a Band-Aid on her arm, those cute cartoon kind, and then one on my own. I said I would, but there wasn't any reason to, neither of us had been cut. I looked up at Ruth and with a gentle laugh, she said, "You don't need to be hurt to have Band-Aids."

Life can be a struggle, and yet it can be so simple. If you don't decide now to redecide, then when? I hope that this book has offered you some concrete options to let go, rethink, review and reevaluate your life mental models. Here are some extra pieces of the puzzle you might consider.

AFTERLIFE

I have this theory about life, death and the afterlife experience.

Wow.
Look at the grass stains
on my skin.
I say, if your knees aren't green
by the end of the day,
you ought to
seriously re-examine your life.

Calvin
Calvin & Hobbes
Bill Watterson, cartoonist

...all acts of healing are
ultimately
our selves healing our Self.

Ram Dass

There are basically two religious philosophies about what life is about and what happens after we die. One is that this is the only life you get. You come here, live it, then die. The afterlife options are heaven and hell and that's it. THE END.

The other is the Karma deal. Karma would say that I am here writing this book and you are here reading it because we didn't get it right the last time we were here, so we had to come back and try it again. If we don't get it right this time, well, we'll be back again. If you *do* get it this time around, you don't have to come back again. You get to go on to some other spiritual plane or something.

Well, I don't know which one of these is right, but I do know this. I am living the *biggest, fullest life* I can possibly create right now. That way I figure I'm covered no matter which philosophy is right! If I only get one try, I'm going to have a good time doing it. If the Karma thing is right, then maybe I won't have to come back again, and that would be just fine with me. I didn't really like those childhood, teen, and 20's years anyway and I certainly don't want to do them again.

TOUCHSTONE:
All of life is a school, with lessons to learn. The faster you learn these lessons, the easier life becomes.

EXERCISE:
Do you know what direction you are taking yourself? Is it worth your effort? Is it exactly where you want to go? Write out the answers to the following questions for more cleaning out and clarity.

1. What are some things I want right now?
   What are some things I want in 3 months?
   . . . in 6 months?
   . . . 1 year?
   . . . 5 years?

2. What would I like to achieve this week?
   What would I like to achieve over the next month?
   ...6 months?
   ...1 year?
   ...5 years?

It's not hard to get enlightened; what is difficult is to keep giving up our sense of the world so that the world can come us on its own terms, with its vast, pitiless, loving intelligence. At the end of the journey, we return to the simplest things with an immense recognition and gratitude....

Stephen Mitchell

The most powerful thing you can do to change the world, is to change your own beliefs about the nature of life, people, reality, to something more positive...and begin to act accordingly.

Shakti Gawain
Creative Visualisation

The sun shines not on us,
but in us.

John Muir

3. What is my most important goal or goals?
   Why is this goal important to me?
4. What interests me the most?
5. What do I value in life?
6. What do I love doing?
7. What brings me joy?
8. What animates me?
9. What helps me feel fulfilled?
10. What other questions are important to me now?
    #1: ....
    #2: ....
    #3: ....

LIFE AND LETTING GO—WITH ALL YOUR MIGHT

Life is a cycle, endings and beginnings, ongoing change and growth. You get "it" or arrive "there" and say, "This is it?" We never get to a final "there" and there is no final "it." After you *shift* into a new mental model, new and other "its" and "there's" will follow.

Life is a struggle due to our attachment to things, people, ideals and beliefs—and our unwillingness to let go. To hold on makes us feel in control and like we know what's happening. To let go is the most courageous, powerful act we can do. To let go means that we don't know; that we don't have control; that we must detach and trust our life process.

Go back through this book reworking exercises now and again. To create and recreate yourself in the spiral of life means *letting go with all your might.*

JUST HOW SIMPLE IT CAN BE!

In closing, I want to share this amazingly simple, yet deeply profound poem by Portia Nelson. It is the most perfect overview of what I have put forth in this book to explain how to let go, shift and make redecisions for life.

Our work is to interpret this
Life/Death/Life cycle,
to live it as gracefully
as we know how,
to howl like a mad dog
when we cannot—and to go on,...

Clarissa Pinkola Estés
Women Who Run
With the Wolves

Thank you for reading my book.

If this book has helped you in any way, I'd love to hear from you.

AUTOBIOGRAPHY IN FIVE SHORT CHAPTERS

1) I walk down the street.
> There is a deep hole in the sidewalk.
> I fall in.
> I am lost . . . I am hopeless.
> > It isn't my fault.
> It takes forever to find a way out.

2) I walk down the same street.
> There is a deep hole in the sidewalk.
> I pretend I don't see it.
> I fall in again.
> I can't believe I am in the same place.
> > But, it isn't my fault.
> It still takes a long time to get out.

3) I walk down the same street.
> There is a deep hole in the sidewalk.
> I see it is there.
> I still fall in . . . it's a habit.
> > My eyes are open
> > I know where I am.
> > It is my fault.
> I get out immediately.

4) I walk down the same street.
> There is a deep hole in the sidewalk.
> I walk around it.

5) I walk down another street.

VIII

Resources

We're just about as happy as we make up our minds to be.

Abraham Lincoln
(1809-1862)

NOTES

Chapter 1
Letting Go
[1] Nisker, Wes "Scoop". *Crazy Wisdom*. Berkeley, CA: Ten Speed Press, 1990, 208.

Chapter 2
ReDecisions for Life
[2] Senge, Peter M. *The Fifth Discipline*. New York, NY: Doubleday, 1990, 8.
[3] Barker, Joel Arthur. *Paradigms, The Business of Discovering the Future*. New York, NY: HarperCollins Publishers, Inc., 1992, 155.
[4] Arrien, Angeles. *Gathering Medicine: Stories, Songs and Methods for Soul-Retrieval*, 13th Annual Common Boundary Conference. Boulder, CO: Sounds True Audio, 1994.

Chapter 3
Mental Model
[5] Senge, Peter M. *The Fifth Discipline*. New York, NY: Doubleday, 1990, 8.
[6] Smith, Adam. *Powers of the Mind*. New York, NY: Ballantine Books, 1975, 19.
[7] Kuhn, Thomas S. *Structure of Scientific Revolutions*. Chicago, IL: University of Chicago Press, 1970.

Chapter 4
Change
[8] Thoele, Sue Patton. *The Courage to be Yourself, A Woman's Guide to Growing Beyond Emotional Dependence*. Nevada City, CA: Pyramid Press, Inc. 1988, 55.
[9] Adapted from: "People In Transition", John D. Adams and Sabina A. Spencer in an article found in, *The Insider*, A Career Information Resource for the Higher Education Community.

Chapter 5
Transitions
[10] Bridges, William. *Managing Transitions, Making the Most of Change.* Reading, MA: Addison-Wesley Publishing Company, 1991.
[11] ibid
[12] ibid
[13] Bridges, William. *Transitions.* Reading, MA: Addison-Wesley Publishing Company, 1980, 13.

Chapter 6
The Shadow
[14] Helmstetter, Shad. *What to Say When You Talk to Yourself.* New York, NY: Pocket Books/Simon & Schuster, Inc., 1982.
[15] ibid
[16] Johnson, Robert A. *Owning Your Own Shadow, Understanding the Dark Side of the Psyche.* New York, NY: HarperCollins Publishers, 1991, 8.
[17] Fox, Matthew. *Illuminations of Hildegard of Bingen.* Santa Fe, NM: Bear & Company, Inc., 1985, 13.
[18] Osborne-McKnight, Juilene. *Parabola, The Magazine of Myth and Tradition.* Article "Resistance to the Call". New York, NY: The Society of the Study of Myth and Tradition, Inc., Spring 1994, 20.
[19] Helmstetter, Shad. *What to Say When You Talk to Yourself.* New York, NY: Pocket Books, 1982.

Chapter 7
The ReDecisions 11-Stage Model
[20] Joseph Campbell, *The Hero's Journey.* New York, NY: HarperCollins, 1990, 122.

Chapter 8
Enlightenment and Endarkenment: The Arrows
[21] Johnson, Robert A. *Owning Your Own Shadow, Understanding the Dark Side of the Psyche.* New York, NY: HarperCollins Publishers, 1991, 75.

Chapter: 9
STAGE 1: Beliefs
[22] Chopra, Deepak. *Ageless Body, Timeless Mind.* Niles, IL: Nightingale-Conant Corporation, 1994.
[23] Ibid

Chapter 10
STAGE 2: The Event

[24] Borysenko, Joan. *Minding the Body, Mending the Mind*. New York, NY: Bantam Books, 1987, 94.

[25] Chopra, Deepak. *Ageless Body, Timeless Mind*. Niles, IL: Nightingale-Conant Corporation, 1994.

Chapter 11
STAGE 3: The Question

[26] Borysenko, Joan. *Minding the Body, Mending the Mind*. New York, NY: Bantam Books, 1987, 94.

[27] Brandon, Nathaniel. *The Six Pillars of Self-Esteem*. New York, NY: Bantam Books, 1994.

Chapter 14
STAGE 6: Doubt and Fear

[29] Lori Starbuck Sarnella.

[30] Lisa Obroslinski.

[31] Borysenko, Joan. *Fire in the Soul, A New Psychology of Spiritual Optimism*. New York, NY: Warner Books, Inc., 1993, 62.

[32] ibid. 26-27

Chapter 22
Intellect, Insight and Wisdom

[33] Bridges, William. *Transitions*. Reading, MA: Addison-Wesley Publishing Company, 1980, 112.

[34] Borysenko, Joan. *Fire in the Soul, A New Psychology of Spiritual Optimism*. New York, NY: Warner Books, Inc., 1993.

[35] Maslow, Abraham. *Toward a Psychology of Being*. New York, NY: Van Nostrand Reinhold, 1968.

BIBLIOGRAPHY

BOOKS

An Adult Child's Guide to What's "Normal", John Friel, PhD & Linda Friel, MA

The Aquarian Conspiracy, Marilyn Ferguson

The Art of Self-Sabotage: Adult Children in the Workplace, Janet Geringer Woititz, EdD (May have a new title)

The Art of the Possible: A Compassionate Approach to Understanding the Way People Think, Learn & Communicate, Dawna Markova, PhD

As A Man Thinketh and *As A Woman Thinketh*, James Allen

The Assertive Option: Your Rights And Responsibilities, Lange and Jakubowski

Be-Good-To-Yourself Therapy, Cherry Hartman (*Wonderful little book!!*)

Beginning to See, Sujata

Being A Man, Patrick Fanning & Matthew McKay, PhD

Boundaries and Relationships, Charles Whitfield, MD

Care of the Soul, Thomas Moore

Choices for Success: Your Happiness is in Your Hands, Judith Orloff-Falk and Peg Doubleday

Choices, and *What To Say When You Talk To Yourself*, Shad Helmstetter (inquire about his many books)

The Circle of Life: Rituals from the Human Family Album, Cohen Publishers, Inc.

The Courage to be Yourself, Sue Patton Thoele

Courage to Change: A Paradigm for Success, Shirley Summer

The Courage To Grieve, and *You Don't Have To Suffer*, Judy Tatelbaum

The Dance of Anger, and *The Dance of Intimacy*, Harriet Goldhor Lerner, PhD

Dark Night of the Soul: St. John of the Cross, Translated and Edited by E. Allison Peers

The Deeper Wound, Recovering the Soul from Fear and Suffering, Deepak Chopra

The *Elf-help* book series by Michael Joseph & R.W. Alley, Abbey Press

Enhancing Self-Concept In Early Childhood, Dr. Shirley Samuels

Enough Is Enough, Carol Orsborn

Feel the Fear and Do It Anyway and *Opening Our Hearts To Men,* Susan Jeffers, PhD

Getting Unstuck: Breaking through Your Barriers to Change, Dr. Sidney B. Simon

Guilt is the Teacher, Love is the Lesson, Fire in the Soul, and *Minding the Body, Mending the Mind,* Joan Borysenko, PhD

Happiness is a Choice, Barry Neil Kaufman

How To Be Your Own Best Friend: How To Take Charge Of Your Life, Mildred Newman & Bernard Berkowitz

How to Enjoy Your Life in Spite of It All, and *A Conscious Person's Guide To Relationships,* Ken Keyes

How to Raise Your Self-Esteem, To See What I See And Know What I Know, and *The Six Pillars of Self-Esteem,* Nathaniel Branden

How To Survive the Loss of a Love, Colgrove, Bloomfield & McWilliams

The Indispensable Woman, Ellen Sue Stern

The Joseph Campbell Companion: Reflections on the Art of Living, Selected and Edited by Diane K. Osborn

The Knight in Rusty Armor, Robert Fisher

Life-Changes: How Women Can Make Courageous Choices, Joan Hatch Lennox & Judith Hatch Shapiro

Life 101, The Portable LIFE 101 and *Do It! Let's Get Off Our Buts,* John-Roger & Peter McWilliams

Living with Vision: Reclaiming the Power of the Heart, Linda Marks

Love Is Letting Go Of Fear, Gerald G. Jampolsky, MD

Love, Medicine & Miracles, Dr. Bernie Siegel (and his other many books and tapes)

Making Our Lives Our Own, Marilyn J. Mason, PhD

The Male Mid-Life Crisis: Fresh Starts after 40, Nancy Mayer

Mastering the Winds of Change: Peak Performers Reveal How to Stay on Top in Time of Turmoil, Erik Olesen

Mastery, George Leonard

Mind as Healer/Mind as Slayer, K.R. Pelletier

Oh, the Places You'll Go!, Dr. Seuss

Old Patterns, New Truths: Beyond the Adult Child Syndrome, Earnie Larsen

On Death and Dying: To Live Until We Say Goodbye, Elisabeth Kubler-Ross

Overcoming Indecisiveness, and *The Anger Book*, Theodore Issac Rubin, MD

Overcoming the Fear of Success, Martha Friedman

Of Course You're Angry, (about living in an alcoholic home), Gayle Rosellini & Mark Worden

Passages: Predictable Crises of Adult Life, Pathfinders: Overcoming the Crises of Adult Life and Finding Your Own Path to Well-Being, Gail Sheehy

Passions: How to Manage Despair, Fear, Rage, and Guilt and Heighten Your Capacity for Joy, Love, Hope and Awe, Dr. Georgia Witkin

The Places That Scare You, A Guide to Fearlessness in Difficult Times, Pema Chödrön

Revolution From Within: A Book of Self-Esteem, Gloria Steinem

Risking, David Viscott, MD

Rituals for Our Times: Celebrating, Healing and Changing Our Lives and Our Relationships, Evan Imber-Black, PhD, & Janine Roberts, EdD

The Road Less Traveled, M. Scott Peck

Running On Empty: Meditations for Indispensable Women, Ellen Sue Stern

Seasons of a Man's Life, Daniel Leninson

Seven Habits Of Highly Effective People, Stephen R. Covey

Slay Your Own Dragons, Nancy Good

The Soap Opera Syndrome, Joy Davidson, PhD

The Superwoman Syndrome, Shaevitz

Taming Your Gremlin: A Guide to Enjoying Yourself, Richard D. Carson

The Secret of the Shadow, The Power of Owning Your Whole Story, Debbie Ford

The 10 Greatest Gifts I Give My Children, Steve Vannoy

There's A Hole In My Sidewalk: the Romance of Self Discovery, Portia Nelson (book of poetry)

Tibetan Wisdom for Living & Dying, Sogyal Rinpoche

Too Good for Her Own Good, Claudia Bepko and Jo-Ann Krestan

Transitions: Making Sense of Life's Changes and *Managing Transitions: Making the Most of Change*, William Bridges

Wake-up Calls: You Don't have to Sleepwalk through Your Life, Love, or Career!, Eric Allenbaugh, PhD

What You Think of Me is None of My Business, Terry Cole-Whittaker

When Bad Things Happen to Good People, Rabbi Harold Kushner

When Things Fall Apart, Heart Advice for Difficult Times, Pema Chödrön

When I Say NO, I Feel Guilty, Manual J. Smith, PhD

The Woman's Book of Courage, Sue Patton Thoele

Women Who Run With the Wolves, Clarissa Pinkola Estés

Woulda, Coulda, Shoulda, Dr. Arthur Freeman & Rose DeWolf

Wouldn't Take Nothing For My Journey Now, Maya Angelou

MOVIES AND VIDEOS WITH A MESSAGE

❧ The Beauty and the Beast (Animated 1991)

❧ A Brief History of Time
The life story of Stephen Hawking, physicist and victim of Lou Gehrig's disease

❧ Big

❧ Biographies of the life of Helen Keller

❧ Cast Away

❧ The Dream Team

❧ Fearless

❧ Flashdance

❧ Gladiator

❧ Groundhog Day

❧ It Could Happen To You

❧ It's Not What Happens To You, It's What You Do About It.
The life story of W Mitchell, international speaker/author, living life fully after numerous devastating accidents and life transitions. Order from www.wmitchell.com.

❧ Joe Versus the Volcano

❧ Mrs. Doubtfire

❧ My Life

❧ Passionfish

❧ Rudy

❧ Schindler's List

❧ Shadowlands
Story of C.S. Lewis' life/love

❧ Shirley Valentine
Mid-life Crises: Adult

❧ The Thornbirds

❧ Time Bandits

...the best results will come to those who make a commitment to evolve.

Paula Peisner Coxe
*Finding Peace:
Letting Go and Liking It*

About the Author
Kim Wolinski, MSW

As a Self-Management consultant, Life Strategist, speaker, trainer, and educator Kim Wolinski specializes in change, transition, stress management and self-directed learning. She works internationally with individuals, organizations and groups to help identify blocks and limits to growth and change. She then assists her clients in developing and taking action on effective life/work ReDecisions.

Go to **www.ReDecisionsInstitute.com** for details on the following products, books, ebooks, tapes, CD's and more.

PROFESSIONAL SPEAKING
Book Kim for your upcoming event.

LIFE STRATEGIST, COACHING AND CONSULTING
By phone or in person.

COACHING AND TRAINING FOR THE PROFESSIONAL SPEAKER, TRAINER and/or CONSULTANT

You can be a great presenter, but if you really want to have a great career as a professional speaker, then you will need to understand and build a business. Learning the right way to run it the first time will save a lot of time, money and frustration.

The workbook *The Nuts & Bolts of the Business of Professional Speaking* is available separately.

COACHING AND TRAINING FOR THE BEGINNING WRITER and/or PUBLISHER

It could never be a better time to be a writer and create passive income in new creative forms.

CONTACT:
    ReDecisions Institute   303-744-8076
    PO Box 6149
    Longmont, CO 80501   KimWolinski@msn.com
          www.ReDecisionsInstitute.com

Order Information

To obtain extra copies of *Letting Go With All Your Might*: *A guide to life transitions, change, choices & effective redecisions,* fill out the following or go to www.ReDecisionsInstitute.com.

Name_____

Company _____

Shipping Address _____

City_____ St _____ Zip Code_____

Phone (day)_(_____)_____

    Email _____

Quantity _____ X $18.95   = _____

       (Colorado res. add 4.3%) Tax = _____

S&H $5.00 per book   = _____

TOTAL AMOUNT ENCLOSED: $ _____

Make check payable to *ReDecisions Institute*

Go to web site for credit card option,

www.ReDecisionsInstitute.com

_____Quantity discounts available upon request_____

Mail order to:

    ReDecisions Institute

    PO Box 6149 ♦ Longmont, CO 80501

    (Outside USA orders, call 303-744-8076)

Questions? Email KimWolinski@msn.com,
or call ReDecisions Institute at 303-744-8076.
Go to www.ReDecisionsInstitute.com
to order this and other products.

Printed in the United States
17785LVS00001BB/21-44